by Komako Ishigaki

translated by John Clark

HOIKUSHA

CONTENTS

Names of Parts 5
Works: Standing Hyogo (Tate Hyogo) 2
        Long Hanging Tress (Sui Hatsu) 6
        Bead-tied (Tama Musubi) 10
        Back-tied Long Hanging Tress (Neyui Suihatsu) . 14
        Sedge Hat (Sugegasa) 18
        Shimada Topknot (Shimada) 22
        Silk Wadding Hat (Wata Boshi) 26
        Shimada Maidservant (Yakko Shimada) 30
        Woman with a Kerchief (Zukin no Onna) 34
        Maid's Head-scarf (Osome Boshi) 38
        Courtesan's Back-tied Long Hanging Tress
           (Neyui Suihatsu: Yujo) 42
        Palace Style (Gosho-fu) 46

    Loop Topknot (Karawamage) 50
    Hyogo Nape Topknot (Nesagari Hyogo) 54
    Katsuyama Topknot (Katsuyamamage) 58
Genre Figures in Landscape:
    Fashions and How to Make Dolls from them . . . 62
    Fashions in the Edo Period 64
    Making Small Dolls 65
Matching Kimono and Obi with Japanese Paper
    and the Patterns of Japanese Kimonos 82
Japanese Folk Paper Dolls 'Anesama' 98
Making Large Dolls in detail 100
One-Woman Show 116
Paris Exhibition 121
Appendix: Japanese Paper Shops 124

Cover Photo: Shimada Topknot

JAPANESE PAPER DOLLS

by Komako Ishigaki

translated by John Clark

© All rights reserved. No. 32 of Hoikusha's Color Books Series. Published by Hoikusha Publishing Co., Ltd., 8-6, 4-chome, Tsurumi, Tsurumi-ku, Osaka, 538 Japan. ISBN 4-586-54032-X. First Edition in 1976. 7th Edition in 1994. Printed in JAPAN

Preface

The dolls gathered in this book were chosen with the way of making them simple enough for beginners. In the larger dolls which are 15cm high, I tried to adopt the fashions and hair styles only from the one hundred year interval around the end of the 17th century, the period when costume was at its most gorgeous. These dolls do not have sleeves attached following the example of the 'Anesama' (Japanese old paper dolls). I have tried to use new silk-screen printed papers in order to bring out the beauty of the costume and have avoided the old fashioned stencil-dyed papers with their mellowed colours. I have also used papers with a gold pattern on a monochrome ground for the obi (kimono sash) to bring to life the colours of the kimono design. For the lining of the kimono I have tried to choose plain colour tone from solid-colour folk art papers. In any case I avoid papers difficult to obtain and use papers being marketed in Japan.

The smaller dolls which are 7cm high are in the fashion of the mid-19th century. I tried attaching sleeves to the smaller dolls in order to give them movement. The materials I used for the kimono are hand-buffed plain paper and modern striped stencil-dyed paper. With this period the pattern on women's kimonos becomes small and the width of the obi increases. I used the same obi as in the larger dolls with coloured plain brocade, that is paper with a gold pattern on a monochrome ground. But you may enjoy devising things using the papers you have to hand as materials without being preoccupied with those mentioned here.

The 30 dolls gathered in this book were newly conceived and made for this book. I used to think that Japanese paper dolls were the only ones with no eyes or nose, but in summer of 1973 I encountered ceramic and wood dolls from Scandinavian without them.

Standing Hyogo

This doll has the costume of a courtesan with a comb and ornamental hairpin inserted in the hair. It appears complicated with a lot of decoration when seen by an amateur, but the opposite is the case simple dolls being the ones difficult to make. The obi which began to be fashionable from about the mid-17th century is rather showily done, tied in the way called the 'playing-card' knot. 'Standing Hyogo' is the name of the doll's hair style.

3

Please refer to pages 100–115 for the way of making this doll where it is explained in detail as the typical case of doll-making.

(Note: The unit of the numbers used for the patterns in this book is centimeter.)

Names of the parts

Long Hanging Tress

The long hanging tress is hair which drops down at the back (refer to page 5). The hair is tied by a flat paper braid in the middle between the forelock and the long hanging tress. The paper braid is a tie used for tying up the hair topknot. It was used during ancient times in the 9th century when it was of thread and twisted paper string. The flat paper braid used paper in stead of cord as now.

The obi tying is called the 'Kichiya' knot where the 'playing card' knot is tied deep with weights attached to each tip. It is the one tied at about the end of the 17th century in Kyoto by Uemura Kichiya, the Kabuki actor of female parts, and seems to have been the fashion at the time.

7

1. Hair

```
| long hanging tress |
|      forelock      |
|     back hair      |
```
12 (height) × 16 (width)

3. Rear obi
— glue margin

2. Obi

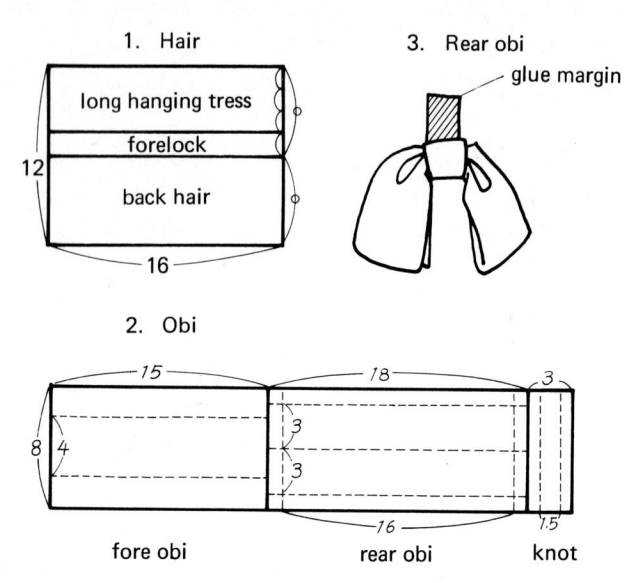

- 15 — fore obi (8 × 4)
- 18 — rear obi (16, with 3/3 markings)
- 3 — knot (1.5)

Making the face   Make the faces of all dolls with reference to that of the 'Standing Hyogo' on page 100. This section will thus be ommitted from the dolls which follow.

Making the head   For the backhair and forelock refer to the 'Standing Hyogo' on page 100. Make the paper for doing the forelock into twisted paper string $1/3$ its length and tie it to the twisted paper string of the forelock. Insert this together with the face into the middle of the back hair and arrange it in place. To the knot on the forelock fix the flat paper braid, which is a piece of thin white Japanese paper 0.5 × 2cm folded in two and knotted once. Likewise tie the middle of the length of the hanging tress with a flat paper braid of 0.8cm width, folded in two. Squeeze the ends of the hair through the hand and bring them together.

Making the torso This section will be ommitted from the dolls which follow since it is the same as the 'Standing Hyogo' on page 100.

Making and dressing the kimono Make and dress the kimono in the same way as the 'Standing Hyogo' on page 100, using the paper pattern A on page 102.

Making and attaching the obi After folding the rear obi to the measurements' width, arrange the angle on both sides and fold the length in two so that the right side will form a loop. Next take a pleat in the middle, wrap round it the paper for the knot and make the shape in diagram 3. Stick this overlap width to the back of the doll, close the fore obi and glue it at the back.

Finishing The finishing is the same as the 'Standing Hyogo' on page 100.

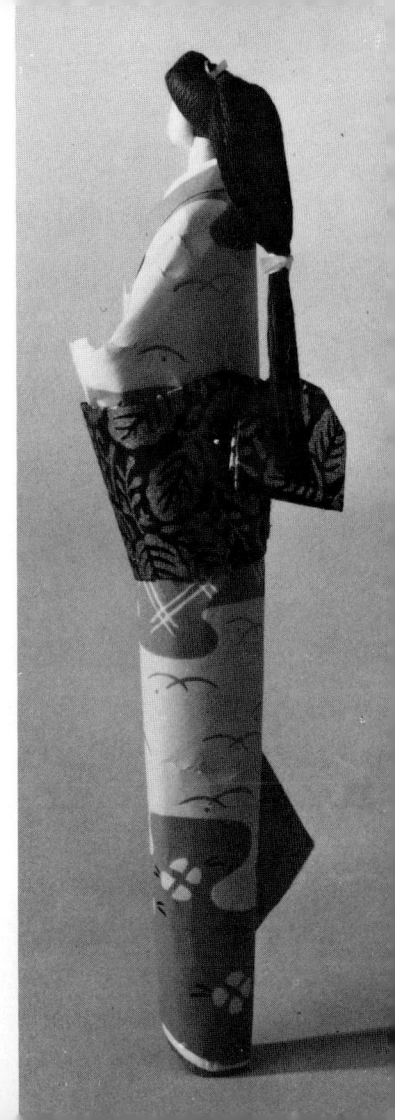

Bead-tied

'Bead-tied' is a hairstyle which was in fashion in the 1680's. The hair left from the forelock was tied in the middle on the back, at the time generally with a flat paper braid. It was a hairstyle tied by courtesans in addition to ordinary women. The obi-tying is with the 'Kichiya' knot.

In those days the obi was first tied on both sides as well as in the front, but tying at the sides declined. Tying in front eventually died out in the latter half of the 17th century, and rear-tying alone developed. In effect obi-tying developed so as to relieve the monotony of the wadded silk figure and produce an original costume beauty.

11

1. Hair

```
         Bead-tied         ) A + 0.5
         forelock          )
  12                        
         back hair         ) A
              16
```

2. Bead-tied

3. Obi

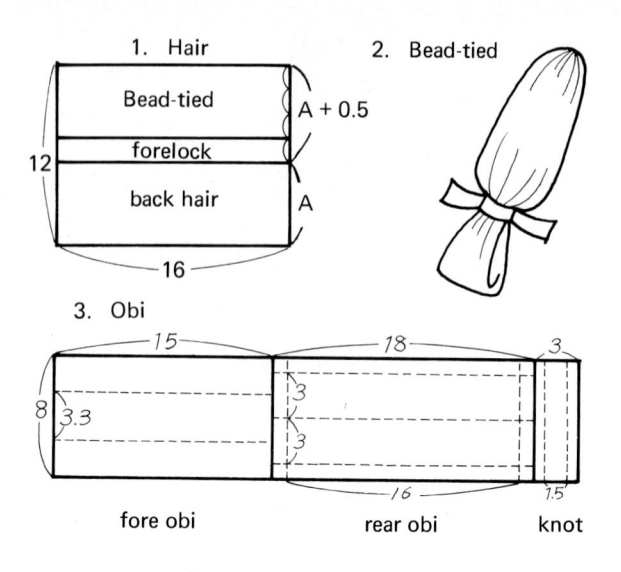

```
     15              18           3
  8 ) 3.3         3                
                  3                
                    16          1.5
    fore obi      rear obi       knot
```

Making the head The back hair and the forelock are the same as the 'Standing Hyogo' on page 100. Make the paper for the 'Bead-tied' hair into twisted paper string to a third of the length. Insert it into the back hair together with the twisted paper string for the face and forelock, and wind the neck. Bend the paper 2.5cm in from the bottom and bundle it up. Tie it with a flat paper braid of thin white Japanese paper, 1.2cm in width folded in two (see diagram 2). Glue the rear of the back hair and steady the bead-tied hair. Attach the forelock as tied with a flat paper braid the same as the Long Hanging Tress on page 6.

Making and dressing the kimono Make and dress the kimono using the paper pattern A the same as the 'Standing Hyogo'.

Making and attaching the obi Making and attaching are the same as the 'Long Hanging Tress' on page 6.

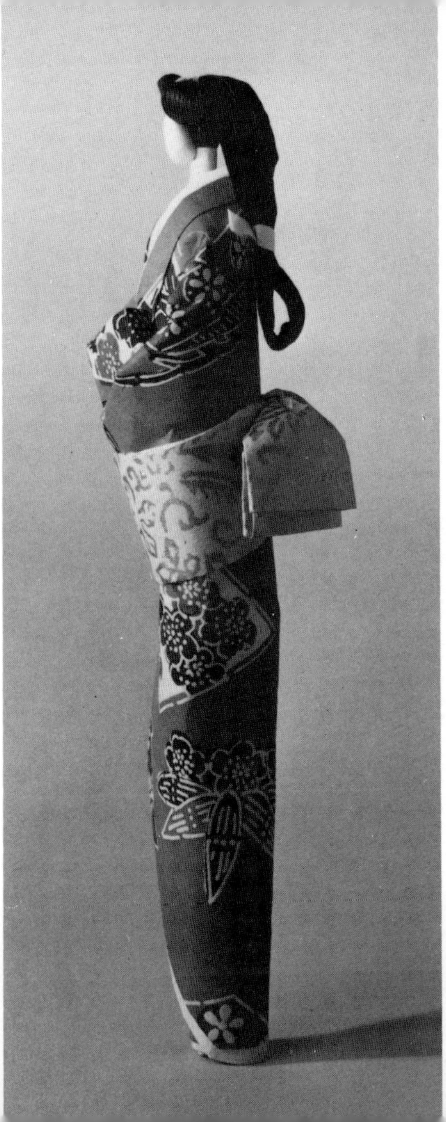

Back-tied Long Hanging Tress

This was the dress of ordinary girls. The style of hair hanging down at the back and tied at the roots was done from the latter half of the 16th century. The roots of the hair are tied with a flat paper braid and the obi is the 'Kichiya' knot.

15

1. Hair

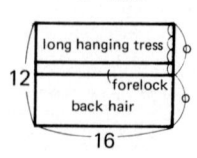

- long hanging tress
- 12
- forelock
- back hair
- 16

2. Pattern B

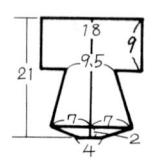

- 18
- 9.5
- 9
- 21
- 7 7
- 4 2

3. Slit for shoulder line

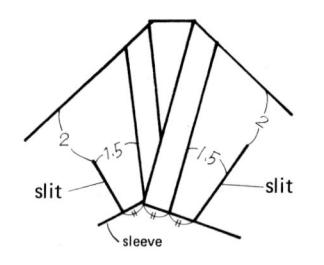

- 2
- 1.5
- 1.5
- 2
- slit — slit
- sleeve

Making the head The back hair and forelock are the same as the 'Standing Hyogo'. After folding the width of the long hanging tress in three bring it together naturally and make it into twisted paper string to third of the length. Insert the long hanging tress into the back hair together with the face and the forelock and arrange it in place. Wrap a piece of white paper 0.4cm in width once around the root of the long hanging tress and glue it. In

4. Hem pleat

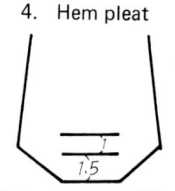

- 1
- 1.5

Take a pleat 0.5cm deep and 3cm long 1.5cm above the hem of the kimono.

5. Obi

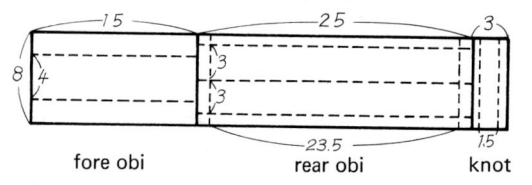

- 15
- 25
- 3
- 8
- 4
- 3
- 3
- 23.5
- 1.5

fore obi | rear obi | knot

16

addition attach on top pieces of paper 0.2 × 2.5cm. Attach a flat paper braid of thin white Japanese paper the same as the forelock for the 'Long Hanging Tress' on page 6.

Making and dressing the kimono
Make the kimono to the same essentials as the 'Standing Hyogo' using the paper pattern B. Loosen the neckband shoulder opening 1cm, and after folding the shoulder line, insert a slit as in diagram 3 and make the sleeveband. Take a pleat in the hem as in diagram 4. Using the slits in diagram 3 dress the upper half of the body as if both sleeves were held to the breast. Dress the lower half of the body with the neckbands of the inner and outer skirts* together and complete the hem line using a hem pleat.

(* Translator's note: The inner and outer skirts refer to the inner and outer flaps of the kimono which are folded left over right for women and men. The kimono is only folded right over left when dressing the dead.)

Sedge Hat

This doll is wearing a hat woven from field sedge and the hair, which cannot be seen properly through the sedge hat, is the Shimada topknot (refer to page 22). The obi tying is the 'Dogwood' knot which flourished in about 1701.

19

1. Hair

topknot
forelock
backhair

12 / 16

2. Topknot

2.3, white paper braid

4. Sedge Hat

front 2.5, back 3, 8cm diameter

3. Obi

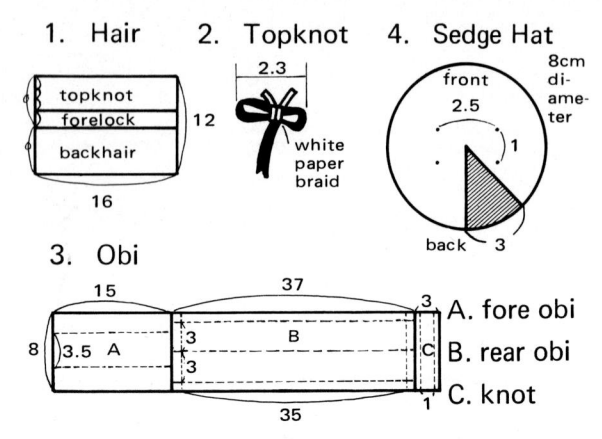

15 — 37 — 3
8 | 3.5 A | 3 | B | C | 35 | 1

A. fore obi
B. rear obi
C. knot

Making the head The back hair and the forelock are the same as the 'Standing Hyogo'. Fold the topknot paper in three to the width of 1.1cm and folding the length to 2cm, make it into the front loop of the Shimada topknot. From there fold the width of the topknot in three again and bend it to the pattern in diagram 2, knot it with a paper braid wrapped round twice. Make the length of the topknot about 2.3cm. Insert the twisted paper string of the topknot, forelock and face into the back hair and make the head.

Making and dressing the kimono Make and dress the kimono to the same essentials as the 'Back-tied Long Hanging Tress' using the paper pattern B on page 16. But insert a sleeveband slit in the outer skirt only and raise the sleeveband of the outerskirt alone (left sleeveband). In the photograph on page 5 the kimono has a pleat taken up, but the kimono is alright without this.

Making and attaching the obi This is the same as the 'Long

Hanging Tress' on page 6.

Making and fitting the Sedge Hat Cut out as in diagram 4, overlap 3cm, and glue it. Open four holes for the cord to pass through. Put cord made from the twisted paper string of thin white Japanese paper into loops on both sides and after dressing the doll with the hat hang a further cord between the loops on both sides and tie under the chin.

Shimada Topknot

The hair is the Shimada topknot of the 1770's which is said to have been begun by the maids of the Shimada relay station on the Tokai highroad. The hairstyle represents the women's topknot of the 18th century of which there are many kinds and whose shape varies according to age, occupation, status and locality. The obi tying comes from Murayama Heijuro and is called the 'Heijuro' knot. It seems to have been fashionable in about 1730.

23

1. Hair

topknot
← forelock
back hair

12 (height), 16 (width)

2. Topknot

white paper braid

white paper (Width of topknot is 0.9cm.)

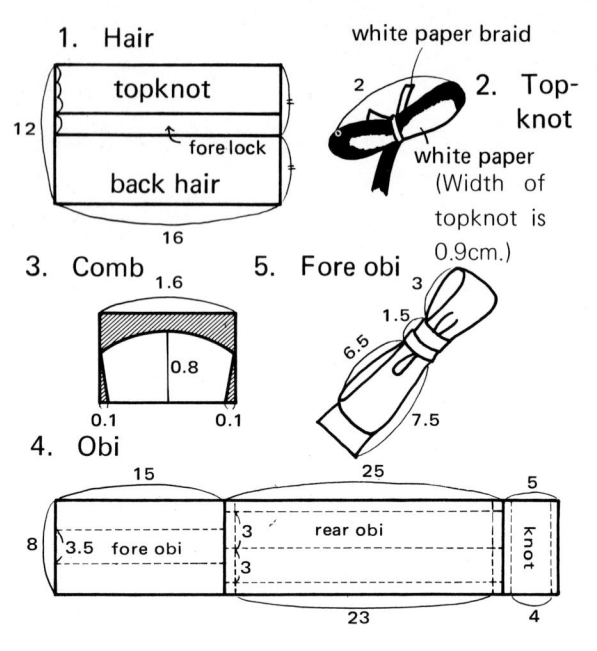

3. Comb

1.6, 0.8, 0.1, 0.1

5. Fore obi

3, 1.5, 6.5, 7.5

4. Obi

15, 25, 5
8, 3.5 fore obi, 3 rear obi, 3, knot
23, 4

Making the head The topknot is the same as the 'Sedge Hat' on page 18, but after glueing a piece of white paper wrapped once around the root of the hair, knot the hair with a white paper braid as in diagram 2. Insert the twisted paper string of the topknot, forelock, and face into the backhair and make the head. Let the root of the hair in the Shimada topknot feel a little loose. Make the comb with gold paper stuck to thick paper as in diagram 3, and insert it into the rear of the forelock.

Making and dressing the kimono Make the kimono using the paper pattern B on page 16, and dress the doll having taken up a pleat in the hem in the same way as the 'Back-tied Long Hanging Tress' on page 14. Do not make a sleeveband in this case and employ the same way of making the arm as the 'Standing Hyogo'.

Making and attaching the obi

Fold the rear obi to the width of 3cm and after putting the corner in order fold the length in two leaving an overlap between the ends of 1cm (7.5 and 6.5cm). Next take up a pleat. Wrap round and glue the paper for the knot of 1.5cm width. Close the fore obi and glue it at the back. Attach the rear obi on top of it at a slight angle.

Silk Wadding Hat

There was a silk wadding hat from the 14th century and with the onset of the 17th century this became headgear reserved for women. Its purpose was in the beginning to keep out the cold but it later came to be used for formal occasions. Among such hats those made of silk wadding in the shape of a narrow boat are called 'boat floss'. The middle is put on the forehead and both ends are tied at the chin. Like the 'Sedge Hat' on page 18 the obi is in the 'Dogwood' knot.

27

1. Hair

- topknot
- back hair
- forelock
- 12
- 16

2. Pattern C

- 18
- 9.5
- 9
- 22.5
- 8 — 8
- 3.5
- 4

3. Obi

- 15 — 32 — 3
- 8 — 3.5
- 3.3
- 3.3
- 30 — 1.3
- fore obi
- rear obi
- knot

4. Rear obi

- 5.8 — 6.5
- 3.5

5. Kimono tuck beneath the obi

- 10
- 4.5
- discard

6. Silk Wadding Hat

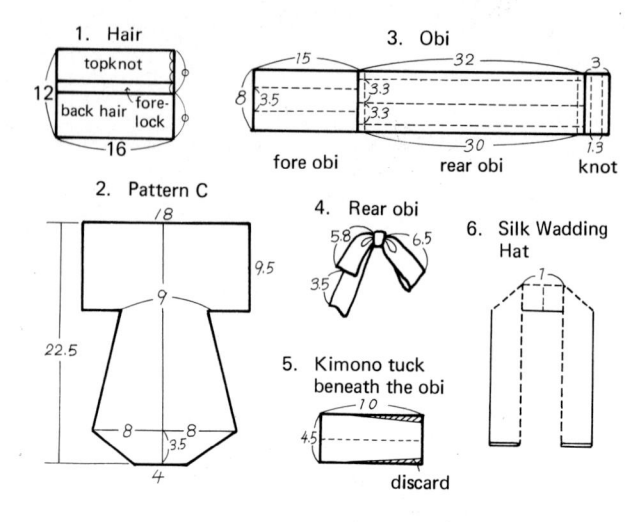

- 1

Making the head The back hair and the forelock are the same as 'Standing Hyogo'. The topknot is to the same essentials as the 'Sedge Hat' on page 18. Make a Shimada topknot 1cm in width by 2.5cm long, and wrap white paper 0.2cm in width twice around the root of the topknot. Leave about 1.5cm on both sides and cut it. Insert the twisted paper string for the topknot, forelock, and face, into the back hair and wind the neck. Insert a comb in the same way as the Shimada topknot on page 22.

Making and dressing the kimono Make the kimono using paper pattern C. With the same outline as the 'Back-tied Long Hanging Tress' on page 14, insert a slit in the innerskirt alone. Take up a pleat in the hem. Hang the sleeveband of the inner skirt only at the breast and dress the doll to the same essentials as the 'Back-tied Long Hanging Tress'.

Making and dressing the obi
Make the rear obi with reference to diagram 4 to the same essentials as the 'Long Hanging Tress' on page 6.

Kimono tuck beneath the obi (Refer to page 5)
Fold the tuck along the dotted line to the measurements in diagram 5 and insert it underneath the obi. Do this having taken up three or four pleats which will fill out a loop in the front of the kimono.

Making and fitting the silk wadding hat Fold thin white paper 3.5 × 10cm in two and after creasing as in diagram 6 put it on the topknot and glue under the chin.

Shimada Maidservant

The hair is one variety of Shimada and is in the style where the root of the topknot was tied prominently. Calling it a Shimada Maidservant was the Kyoto and Osaka way, and in Edo, present day Tokyo, it was called the 'Tall Shimada'.

The obi has the incomplete knot which was fashionable in about 1670. The grounds of the obis of this period have gold brocade, velvet polychrome damask, monochrome damask and figured satin. The colours of brown, light blue, mauve, white and mouse grey were prevalent, and the patterns were mainly of flowers, birds, insects and utensils expressed by dyeing, embroidery and embroidery with metal foil.

31

1. Hair

- topknot
- forelock
- back hair

12 / 16

2. Topknot

white paper braid
white paper

3. Obi

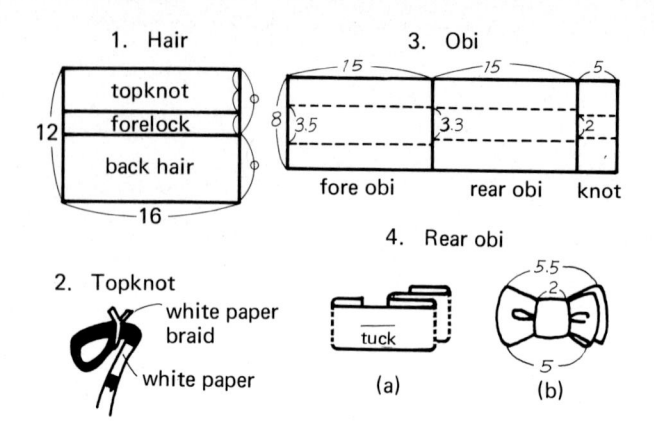

15 — 15 — 5
8 / 3.5 / 3.3 / 2

fore obi | rear obi | knot

4. Rear obi

tuck

(a)

5.5 / 2 / 5

(b)

Making the head The back hair and the forelock are the same as the 'Standing Hyogo'. Make the Shimada topknot with a width of 0.8cm and length of 1.8cm to the same essentials as that on page 22. With reference to diagram 2, wind a piece of white paper 0.9cm in width around the root and fix it with glue; tie a white paper braid over the topknot. Insert the topknot, forelock, and face into the back hair, and wind the neck. Insert a comb in the same way as the 'Shimada Topknot' on page 22.

Making and dressing the kimono Make the kimono and dress it to the same essentials as the 'Sedge Hat' on page 18 using the paper pattern B on page 16. That is, dress it so that only the sleeve of the outer skirt rises.

Making and attaching the obi First close the fore obi and glue it at the back. Make the rear obi as in diagram 4 after folding to the measurements' width. The pleat here is gathered to the same essentials as the rear obi for the 'Long Hanging Tress' on page 6, but leave it rather shallow. Glue the completed rear obi in the middle at the back.

33

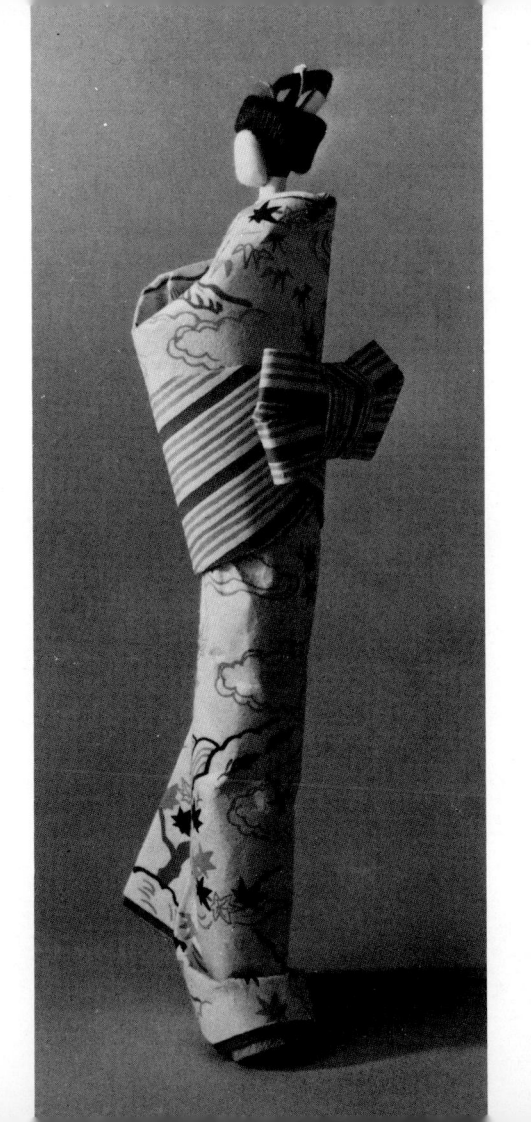

Woman with a Kerchief

The kerchief developed as monks' headgear in the 14th century but became extremely popular in the 16th century. It was especially popular among women as a mode of disguise. Whilst there were also coloured kerchiefs I decided on a white one for this doll, and for the obi decided on the fore knot tied by a middle aged woman. When you do a young woman's obi in the fore knot it becomes the dress of a courtesan.

35

Making the head Arrange the face in place straightway when you have made the back hair. Twist paper into loose paper string and make a small spiral. Glue the spiral on top of the back hair.

Making and dressing the kimono Make the kimono using the paper pattern C on page 29. Without making a slit for the sleeve dress the kimono to the same essentials as the 'Shimada Topknot' on page 22.

Making and attaching the obi Shut the rear obi and glue it at the front. Having folded the fore obi to the measurements' width take up a pleat as in (a) of diagram 3 and make shape (b) after further bending along the dotted line. Wind it round the paper for the knot as in (c). Attach this in front to the middle of the rear obi.

1. Hair

2. Obi

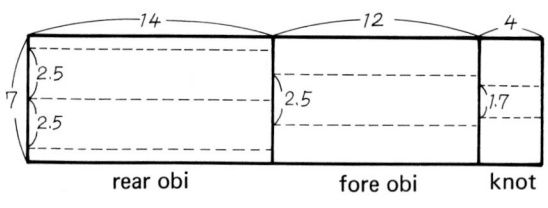

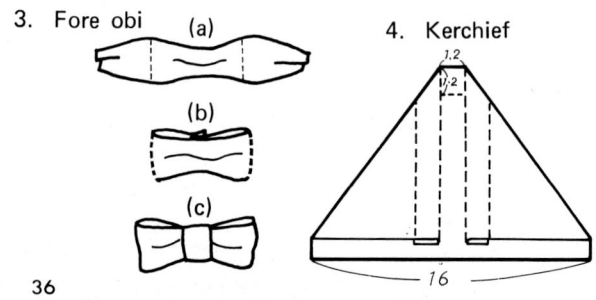

3. Fore obi   (a)
   (b)
   (c)

4. Kerchief

Making and dressing the kerchief
For the kerchief prepare thin paper 9 x 16cm whose colour matches the kimono and obi and put it on the doll having beforehand given it the creases as in diagram 4. Glue the kerchief under the chin while referring to the photograph of the finishing, and harmonize it with the whole body.

Maid's Head-scarf

The maid's head-scarf was fashionable in about 1733 and has this name because the Kabuki actor Segawa Kikunojo used it in the impersonation of a mansion-house maid. In a different name the doll took that of the actor and is called the 'Segawa' head-scarf. Whilst Segawa Kikunojo was an actor of female parts, in his daily life he was also a great success in having put into practice living completely as a woman. The hair is called 'double-loop' or 'double-braided' hair, and is the hair style of married women in Kyoto and Osaka.

39

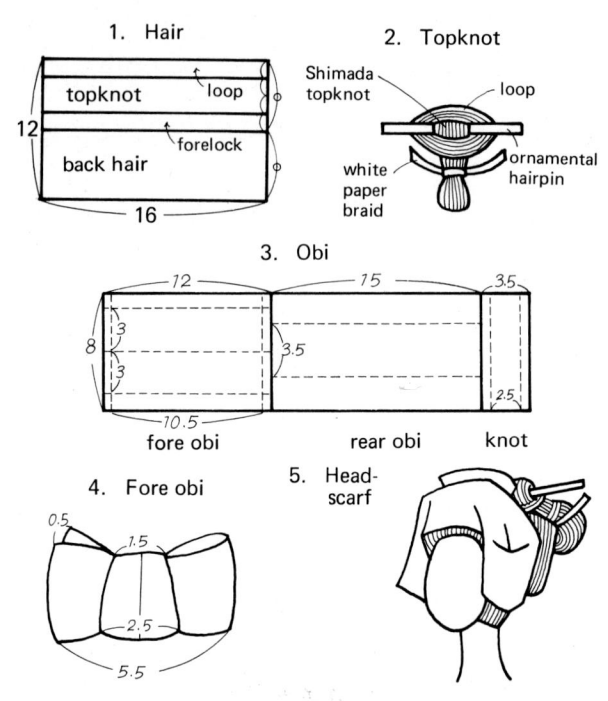

1. Hair

topknot	loop
back hair	forelock

12 / 16

2. Topknot

Shimada topknot, loop, white paper braid, ornamental hairpin

3. Obi

fore obi — 12, 8, 3, 3, 10.5, 3.5

rear obi — 15

knot — 3.5, 2.5

4. Fore obi

0.5, 1.5, 2.5, 5.5

5. Head-scarf

Making the head The back hair and forelock are the same as the 'Standing Hyogo'. For the topknot make first the Shimada topknot, 0.7cm in width and 2cm long, to the same essentials as the Shimada of the 'Sedge Hat' on page 18. Wind around it a piece of white paper 0.2cm in width, and then hang on the Shimada a piece of paper folded to 0.4cm in a loop as in diagram 2. Pass through it an ornamental hairpin 0.3cm by 3.2cm, made from thickgold-coloured paper. Insert the twisted paper string of

40

the topknot, forelock, and face into the back hair, and wind the neck. Insert a comb in the same way as the 'Shimada Topknot' on page 22.

Making and dressing the kimono

Make the kimono using the paper pattern C on page 29, and dress the doll to the same essentials as the 'Shimada Topknot' on page 22.

Making and tying the obi Make the fore obi with reference to the finishing diagram 4 and after closing the rear obi, glue the fore obi in the middle at the front.

Making and dressing the Maid's headscarf

After folding the maid's headscarf to the same essentials and measurements as the 'Silk Wadding Hat' on page 29, put it on the forelock. Test folding to the rear the parts which hang down on both sides and complete the measurements by adjusting the headscarf to the size of the face. Fit the flaps in to make the shape in diagram 5, and glue the hat.

Courtesan's Back-tied Long Hanging Tress

This is the same style as that on page 14 but I have done the bundle of hair thick and showy since this has the dress of a courtesan. The ends of the hair are cut even. The hair style is one originally done up among the wives of the warrior households.

The obi tying is in the 'playing-card' knot. In the Edo period women had all kinds of tastes in obi. From the 1660's the width increased and by the first half of the 18th century it had become 24—27cm, and hence various shapes of obi tying were devised.

43

1. Hair

- long hanging tress
- forelock
- back hair

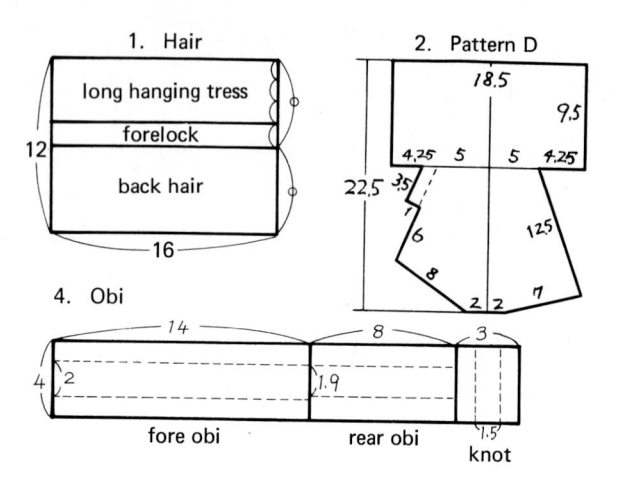

12 | 16

2. Pattern D

18.5, 9.5, 4.25, 5, 5, 4.25, 22.5, 3.5, 7, 6, 8, 2, 2, 7, 12.5

4. Obi

14 — 8 — 3
4 | 2 | 1.9 | 1.5
fore obi — rear obi — knot

Making the head

Make the head with the same outline as the 'Back-tied Long Hanging Tress' on page 14, wind the tress at the root with white paper and attach a flat paper braid to the forelock.

Making and dressing the kimono Make the kimono using the paper pattern D (diagram 2). Since the

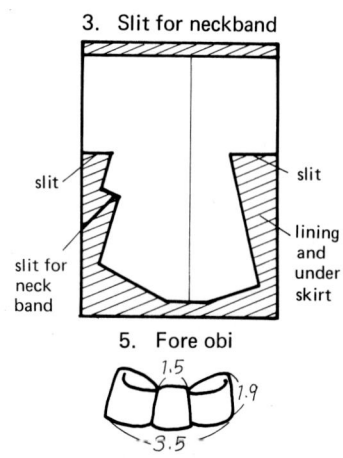

3. Slit for neckband

slit, slit, lining and under skirt, slit for neck band

5. Fore obi

1.5, 1.9, 3.5

44

neckband tip will be made with this pattern, fold the kimono after inserting a slit with reference to diagram 3. The order of folding is the same as the other paper patterns. The essentials for dressing the doll are the same as the 'Standing Hyogo', but dress it comfortably whilst referring to the photograph.

Making and attaching the obi

First close the rear obi and glue it in front. Make the fore obi to the shape in diagram 5 from paper folded to the measurements' width and glue it to the middle at the front.

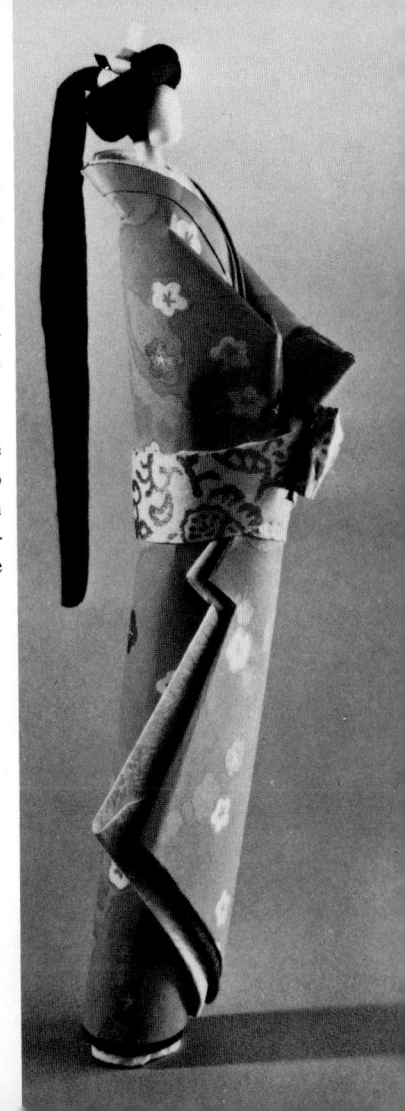

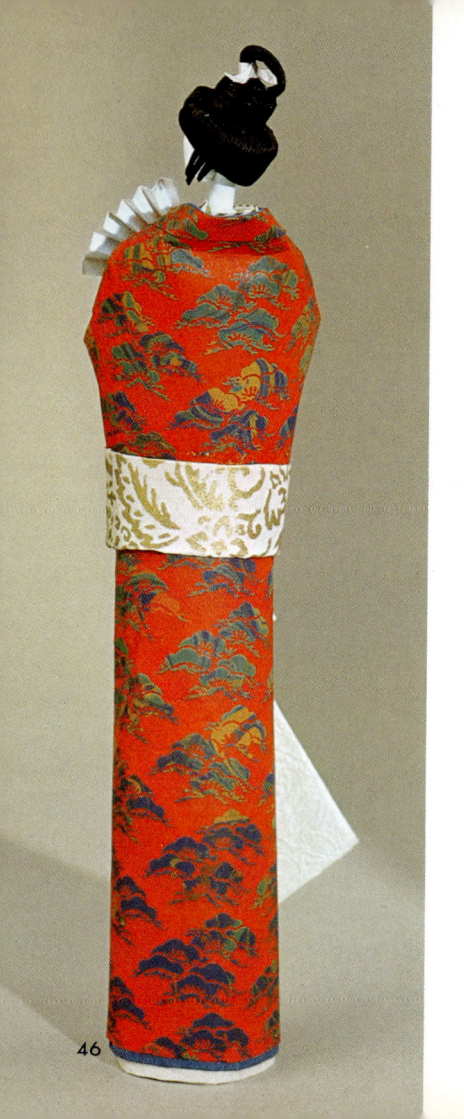

Palace Style

This doll's dress was made with reference to a rather early 'Picture of Beautiful Women of the Kanbun Era'. This picture describes the standing figures of the courtesans of the 1660's and depicts the elegant and showy clothes and the standing hyogo topknot. The origin of these hair styles was in the braided hair of the palace ladies-in-waiting which was fashionable later for the hair of courtesans.

47

1. Hair

topknot	
forelock	
back hair	

12 / 16

3. Fore obi

3 / 2 / 1.2

2. Obi

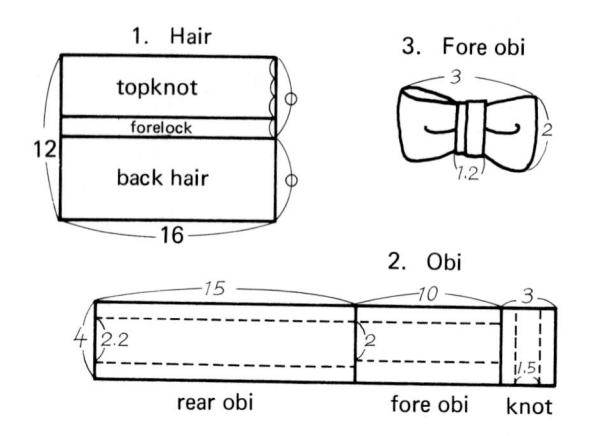

15 / 10 / 3
4 / 2.2 / 2 / 1.5

rear obi — fore obi — knot

Making the head The back hair and forelock are the same as the 'Standing Hyogo'. After bringing the topknot together over its whole length, and leaving about 1cm at the root, tie it with a flat paper braid made from a piece of thin white paper, 0.8cm in width and folded in two. Wrap the hair ends tied by the flat paper braid once around a thick brush, and make the shape for the topknot. Wind in the remainder of the hair to the root of the topknot and fix it with glue. Insert the twisted paper string of the forelock and face into the back hair and wind the neck. Glue the topknot to the back hair. Work the side hair for the decorative loops so that they are properly shaped.

Making and dressing the kimono Make the kimono in the same way as the 'Back-tied Long Hanging Tress' on page 42, using the paper pattern D on page 45, but insert a slit in the under skirt and raise the sleeve. The dressing of the kimono is also to the same essentials as the 'Back-tied Long Hanging Tress' on page 42.

Making and attaching the obi
Make the shape of the obi as in diagram 3. Shut the rear obi, glue it, and attach it to the fore obi in the middle at the front.

Making the fan Fold gold paper, 3 × 4.8cm, in a bellows 0.4cm in width, tie the end with thread, and insert and glue it into the sleeveband.

Loop Topknot

This was fashionable as the hairstyle of courtesans from the end of the 16th century to the beginning of the 17th century and, renamed the Hyogo topknot, seems to have become a topknot reserved for women in the 1610's. Perhaps because the loop topknot was originally a man's topknot the hair is undecorative and is of a very simple shape, gathered upwards. There are many cases with a parted forelock. The obi is narrow in width and tied at the side in front, the width of the torso thus appears larger than usual so giving a grander physical appearance.

51

1. Hair

- topknot
- discard
- paper which winds topknot
- front parted hair
- back hair
- 12
- 16

4. Fore obi

- 1
- 2

3. Obi

- 15
- 6
- 2
- 5
- 2
- 2
- 2
- 4
- 1

rear obi   fore obi   knot

2. Topknot

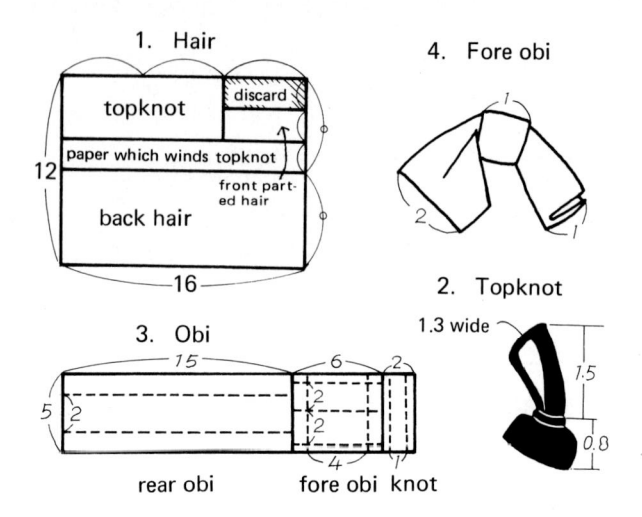

- 1.3 wide
- 1.5
- 0.8

Making the head   Make the topknot and the back hair the same as the 'Standing Hyogo'. The measurements of the topknot are as in diagram 2. Insert the twisted paper of the topknot and face into the back hair and wind the neck. After folding the paper for the front-parted hair in two, put a crease in the middle of the length, glue the peak of the fold, and attach it to the centre of the head. After inserting two slits examine the overall balance and adjust the length.

Making and dressing the kimono   Make and dress the kimono in the same way as the 'Back-tied Long Hanging Tress' on page 42, using the paper pattern D.

Making and attaching the obi   Fold the fore obi to the width of 2cm, and further fold the width in two after arranging the corner. Then give the obi a twist in the middle, wind the paper for the knot at the place where the obi was twisted, close the rear obi and glue it to the front of the doll with a slight inclination to the right. Attach the fore obi on top. Then widen out the end on one side and adjust the shape (refer to diagram 4).

Hyogo Nape Topknot

It seems that the Hyogo nape topknot began to be fashionable in the Yoshiwara or courtesans' quarter of Edo, modern Tokyo, in 1723. The position of the Hyogo topknot was lowered to the back of the head and the topknot became smaller in size.

55

Making the head The back hair and the forelock are the same as the 'Standing Hyogo'. After folding the width of the topknot 0.7cm, fold the length in two whilst giving it roundness with a narrow brush. Next bring together the paper which winds the root and glue it like the shape made in diagram 2. Cut away the surplus underneath the topknot. Insert the twisted paper string of the forelock and face into the backhair and wind the neck. Glue the topknot to the middle of the rear of the back hair. Attach a comb in the same way as the 'Shimada Topknot' on page 22.

1. Hair

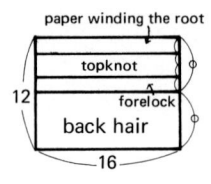

paper winding the root
topknot
forelock
back hair
12
16

2. Topknot

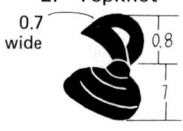

0.7 wide
0.8
7

3. Pattern E

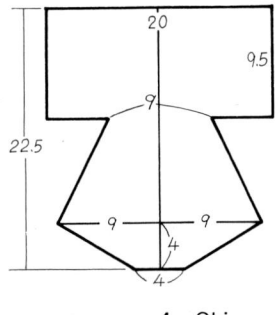

20
9.5
9
22.5
9
9
4
4

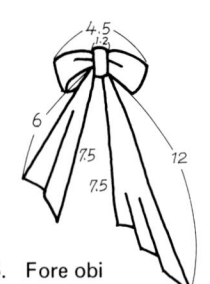

4. Obi

17
30
5
5
rear obi
fore obi
knot

5. Fore obi

4.5
1.2
6
7.5
7.5
12

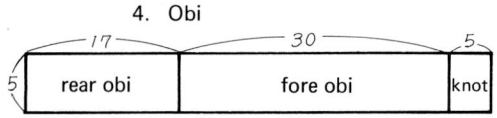

Making and dressing the kimono
Make the kimono using the paper pattern E (diagram 3). The dressing of the kimono is the same as the upper half to the 'Standing Hyogo', and for the lower half combine the outer and inner skirts and fold them together.

Making and attaching the obi
Use hand buffed paper drawn through the hand for the obi paper. Shut the rear obi with a kimono tuck in place beneath it, refer to the 'Silk Wadding Hat' on page 26, and glue it in front. Make the fore obi to the shape in diagram 5 and attach it in the middle at the front.

Katsuyama Topknot

The courtesan Katsuyama first began to tie this topknot in the 1650's. It was not only the hairstyle of courtesans but spread to ordinary women. Since the obi is a courtesan's it is done in the front knot, tied with a showy feeling.

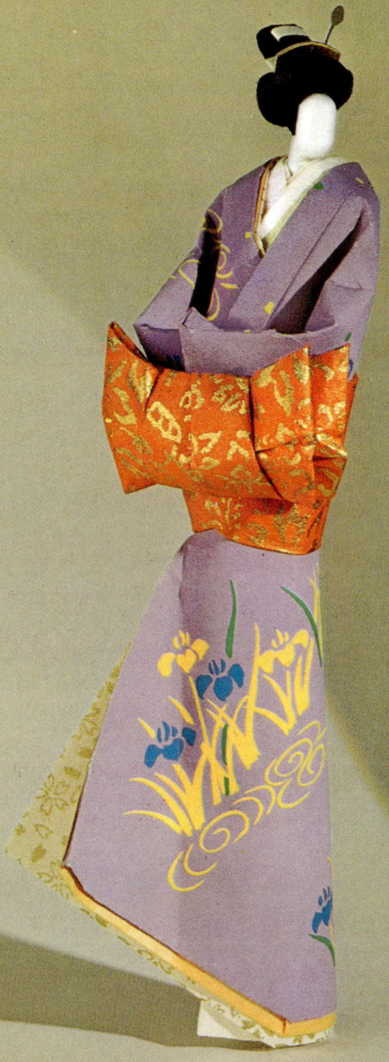

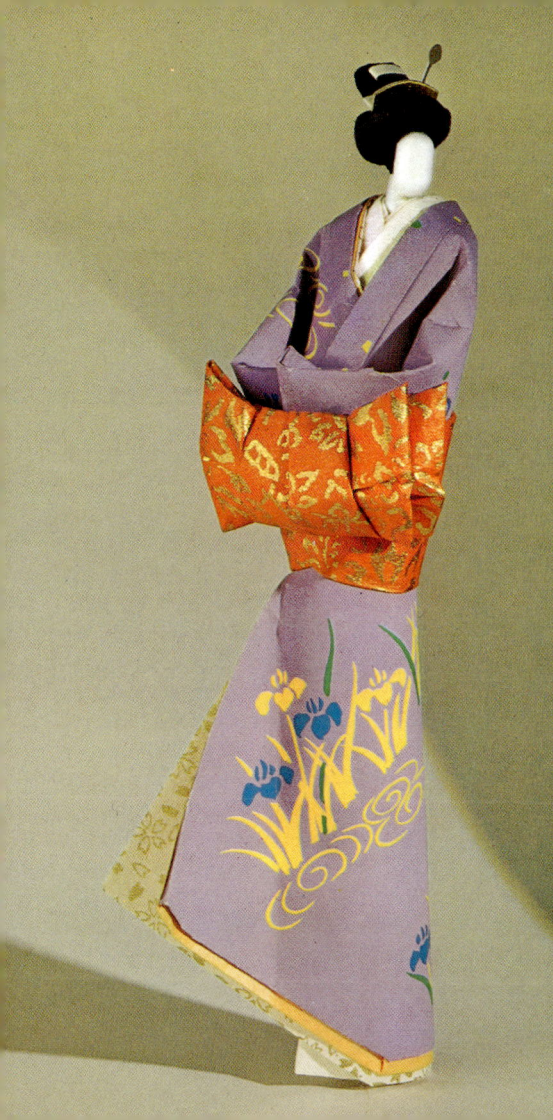

1. Hair

topknot
back hair / forelock
12 × 16

2. Topknot

white paper
twisted paper string
white paper

3. Ornamental hairpin

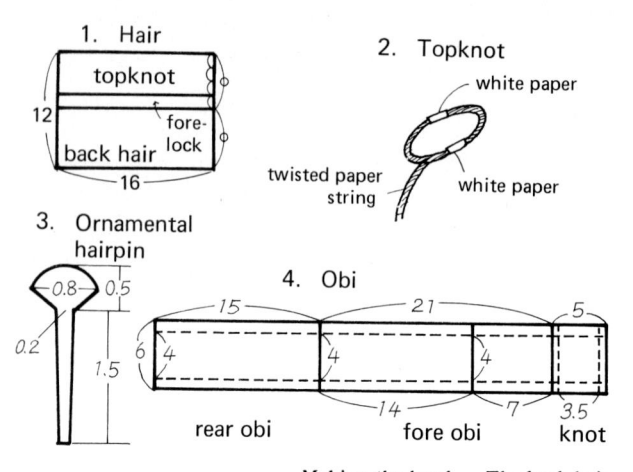

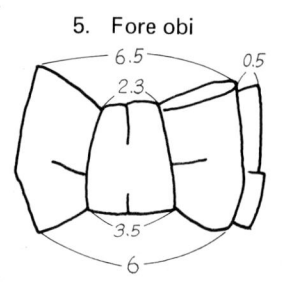

0.8 — 0.5
0.2
1.5

4. Obi

15 — 21 — 5
6 / 4 / 4 / 4
14 — 7 — 3.5
rear obi — fore obi — knot

5. Fore obi

6.5, 0.5, 2.3, 3.5, 6

Making the head The back hair and the forelock are the same as the 'Standing Hyogo'. Fold the topknot in four to 0.7cm of the width, wind it round a thick brush, glue it down and make the remainder into twisted paper string. Wind pieces of white paper 0.4cm in width around the middle of the top and bottom of the topknot and glue them down as in diagram 2. Insert the twisted paper string of the topknot, forelock, and face into the back hair, and wind the neck. Attach a comb in the same way as the 'Shimada Topknot' on page 22. Stick two pieces of gold coloured paper together, make the ornamental hairpin in diagram 3 and insert it. Refer to the photograph for the place to insert the hairpin.

Making and dressing the kimono Make the kimono using the paper pattern E on page 57, and dress it in the same way as the 'Hyogo Nape Topknot' on page 54. Do not take in a kimono tuck.

Making and attaching the obi For the fore obi take up a pleat to the same essentials as the fore obi of the 'Woman with a Kerchief' on page 34, and make the shape in diagram 5. For the doubled-up part lay loops folded to the same shape on top of each other. It will thus be easier to make if you wind around a piece of white paper in readiness, before winding the paper for the knot. Close the rear obi and glue it in front. Attach the fore obi on top of it.

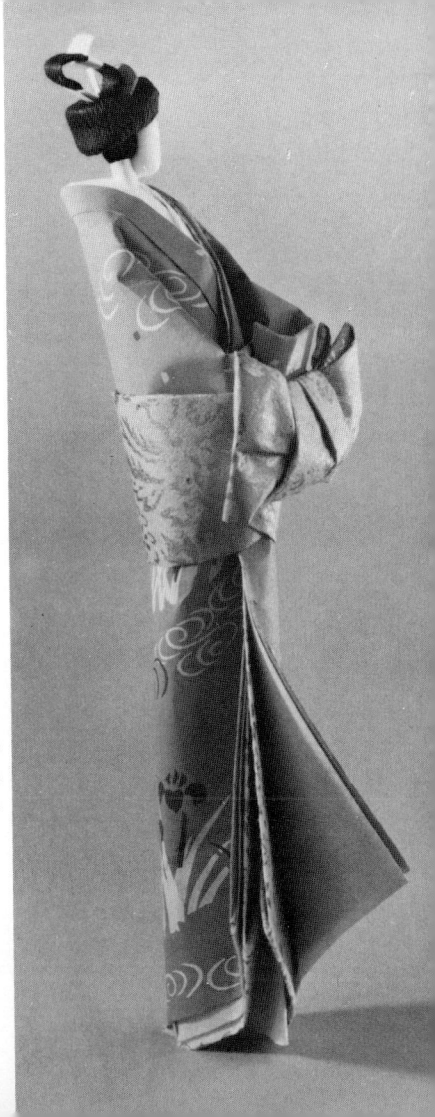

Genre figures in landscapes:
Fashions and how to make dolls from them

Among the Ukiyoe, or pictures of the floating world, I prefer landscapes to pictures of people and I especially like the landscapes of Hokusai (1760–1849) and Hiroshige (1797–1858). I am just struck with admiration at the ingenuity of the composition even if I see these pictures again and again. The bean-shape figures in those landscapes are also fascinating, and I once thought I would try to make dolls of them. I attempted a different method to those up to now, and this method remains at the trial stage.

Woman with a founder's kerchief

Man with a bamboo hat

Man carrying a livery coat

Child with an apron

Man dressed for the Yoshiwara, the courtesan quarter

Fashions in the Edo period (1603—1867)

In the fashions of the 17th century we must not forget the vogue for the haori, a half-length coat. In the early part of the 17th century the length of the haori of the 1730's a haori appeared with the same length as the kimono. Then in the 1750's the short haori appeared worn by the dandies. The short haori was preferred in Edo and the long haori in Osaka. The long haori was also liked most by artisans who probably wore it when they went to visit the courtesans. Among the dolls gathered here I have dressed the 'Retired man' and the 'Man with a Fan' in haoris.

In addition the livery coat, han-ten, may be mentioned as a new and distinctive garment created in this period. Whilst the livery coat was slipped on like the haori, unlike the haori the neckband was not folded back. Men wore it to keep out the cold and women wore it as ordinary dress. The man's livery coat was striped and of crepe or pongee with silk at the back. A replaceable black neckband was sometimes fastened. It was popularly used by women in the 18th century and by about the year 1850 was used almost as much as the haori. Of the dolls in this chapter I have dressed the 'Woman with a Founder's Kerchief' and the 'Man in a Livery Coat' in striped livery coats.

Let me explain here that a 'Founder's Kerchief' is a headgear which wraps the forehead. It is a square with cord loops attached for hanging over the ears, and was mainly worn by women to protect them from the cold being hung over the face from the forehead. It began to be worn from the 1750's and was especially popular in the 19th century, the Meiji period.

From among the other dolls let me mention something about the 'Tipped Ornamental Hairpin'. This was used by maids-in-waiting in the 17th century to arrange long nape hair and the practice also spread among ordinary people. At first the materials used were the shin bones of whales and cranes. Cranes were for the high class articles but from the 1690's kinds of tortoiseshell were used and in the 1720's inlaid lacquer hairpins became more prevalent. These were small at first but from the 1720's the length, thickness and width changed, and in the 1810's huge hairpins were made of 36cm in length.

Making Small Dolls (Example: Katsuyama, page 67)

[Materials]
Kimono: 8 × 17cm, Obi: 3 × 13cm, Wire: 20cm, Absorbent cotton wool: 4 × 8cm, Children's glass marbles: 1.5cm diameter, Japanese paper for the hair: 2.5 × 7cm, Thin white paper: 2.5 × 10cm, Japanese paper for the neckband, the same as the kimono: 1 × 8cm

1. Kimono

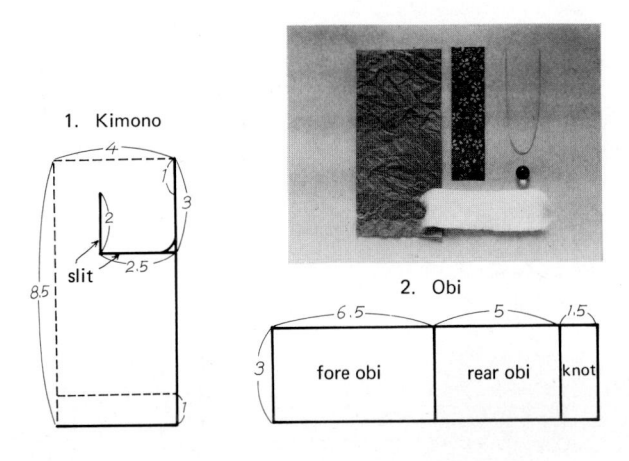

2. Obi

Tipped Ornamental Hairpin

Young child

Man with a burden

Girl in long-sleeved kimono

Katsuyama

Man with a bamboo hat

67

Making the 'Katsuyama'

1 Make round absorbent cotton wool to the same essentials as the 'Standing Hyogo' on page 100, cut off and wrap thin white paper around the cotton wool so making the face. In this case use a piece of thin white paper whose measurements are about 2.5cm in width and 10cm in length. However make this a small face in terms of the whole.

2 Put twisted paper string across the rearside of the face, glue it and cut off the surplus paper.

3 Cut the black Japanese paper for the head to a width of 2.5cm and a length of 4cm, and then crumple the width to 2cm. Wind the crumpled paper three or four times round a toothpick, glue it on the wound part and make the back hair.

4 Glue the back hair around the face taking care that the length of the back hair is the same on both sides.

5 Glue what remains of the back hair and stick it together at the rear part of the head. Cut the part stuck together as in the diagram.

6 Fold in three the width of black Japanese paper, 1cm wide and 2.5cm long, make it into a loop and glue it. This will become the topknot. Glue the loop to the rear part of the head.

7 Fold the width of the kimono in two, and fold the length in two as well. Insert slits agreeing with the measurements of diagram 1 on page 65. Make it round since this part will become the sleeve. When you spread out the kimono with the slits inserted it will be like diagram 7. After extending it fold the hem 1cm.

8 Bend the length of the wire in two, extend the ends to 3.5cm on each side and twist the join in the wire.

9 . Wind the absorbent cotton wool round the wire.

69

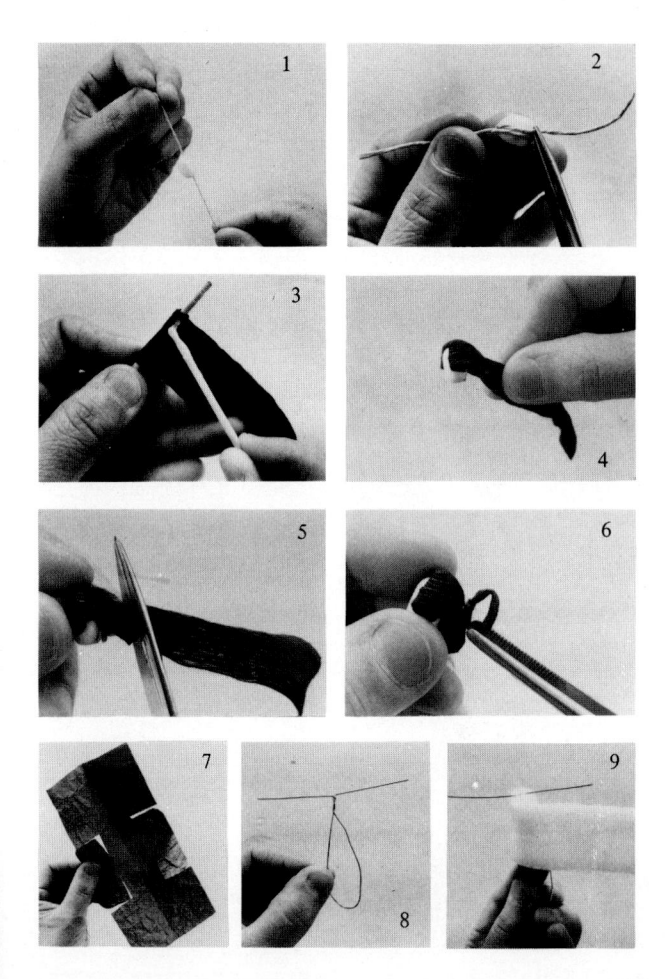

Woman with an apron

Retired man

Woman with umbrella

Child

Child with an apron

10 Rest the wire wound with cotton wool on top of the extended kimono. Now position the widened out part of the wire so that it corresponds to the shoulder ridge of the kimono.

11 Arrange the hem at the front and back and fold the underskirt. Next fold the outerskirt and as you do so fold the edge of the outerskirt in about 0.3cm. Glue the upper side of the outerskirt. Open the sleeve band 1cm and glue beneath the sleeveband.

12 Fold the width of both the fore and rear obi in two. Take up a pleat in the middle of both the width and length of the rear obi and arrange the shape as in the diagram. This is called the 'library' knot.

13 Fold in two the 1.5cm width of paper for the knot, put it in the middle of the rear obi and glue it down. Glue the rear side of the paper for the knot.

14 Attach the rear obi to the back of the doll's torso. Decide on the height of the fore obi and move it round to the back. Glue the fore obi beneath the rear obi.

15 Fold in two 1cm wide paper for the neckband, and insert the edge of the outerskirt into the obi. As a procedure you may also attach the neckband before shutting the obi. The photograph is of the completed neckband attachment.

16 Decide the position of the shoulder and bend the wire so that the arms fall downwards. Arrange it properly so that the shape of the kimono sleeve and so forth is not artificial.

17 Glue the jaw part of the face, and glue the face whilst observing the overall balance.

18 Glue the inner side of the kimono hem in readiness, insert the glass marble and fix it securely. Since the glass marble is inserted in all the small dolls I will omit it from the way of making the last two dolls.

73

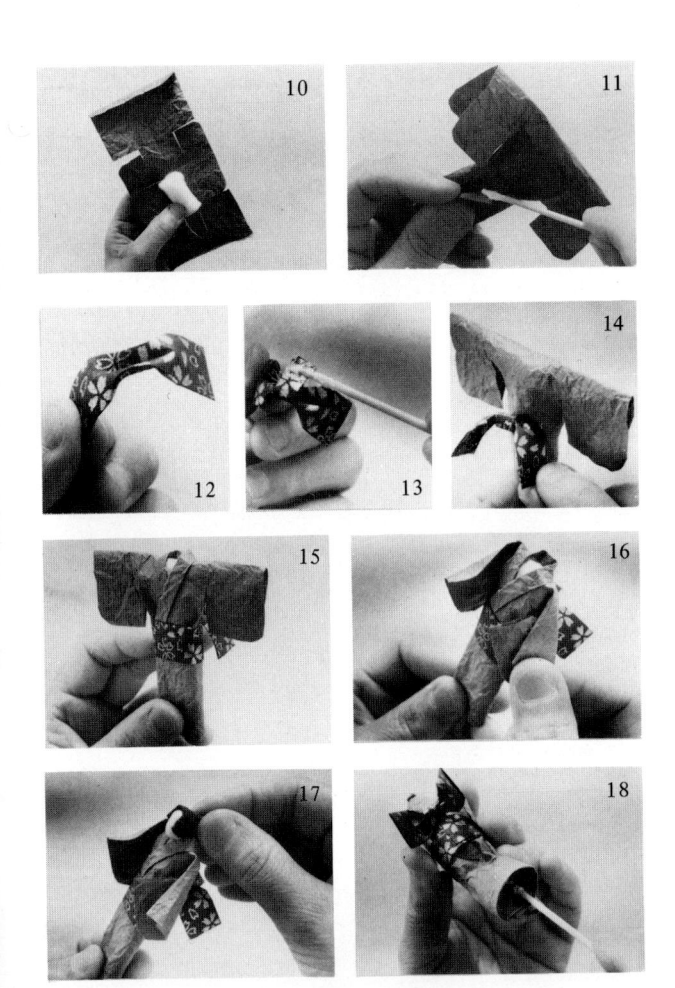

Katsuyama

Man with a fan

Retired man

Tipped Ornamental Hairpin

Woman with a founder's kerchief

Man in a livery coat

Girl with a long-sleeved kimono

75

Making the 'Girl with a Long-sleeved Kimono'

[Materials]
Japanese paper for the hair: 2.5 x 7cm, Kimono: 8 x 17cm, Neckband: 1 x 8cm, Part for winding round the hips: 9x 5.5cm Obi: 4 x 18cm, Some pieces of thin red paper

Making the face   The same as the 'Katsuyama' on pages 68 to 69.

Making the head   The way of making the back hair and the extra back tress is the same as the 'Katsuyama'. After folding in two the topknot paper of 1.5cm in width, make a Shimada topknot 1.3–1.4cm in length, and tie it in the middle with white cotton thread. As you glue this to the rear of the back hair draw some thin red paper through your hands, insert it beneath the topknot and glue them together.

Making and dressing the kimono   The essentials of making and dressing the kimono are the same as the 'Katsuyama'. Because the sleeves are long the horizontal slit in the doll is visible, and so after dressing the kimono fold a 1cm hem on the part of the paper for winding round the hips, and then wind this paper round and attach it. Fold the neckband to a width of 0.5cm and attach it.

Making and attaching the obi   Close the fore and rear obis after folding the width of both in two. First shut the fore obi and glue it at the back. Make a 0.9cm overlap between both ends and then fold the rear obi in two. Wrap paper for the knot round it, folded in two, and glue it to the back.

1. Kimono

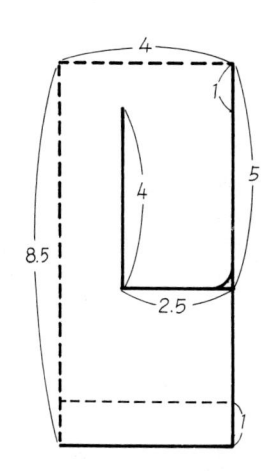

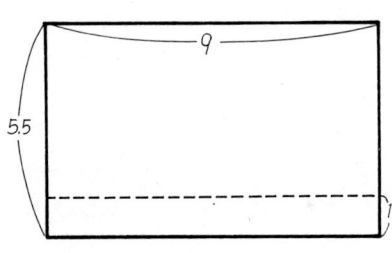

2. Part for winding round the hips

3. Obi

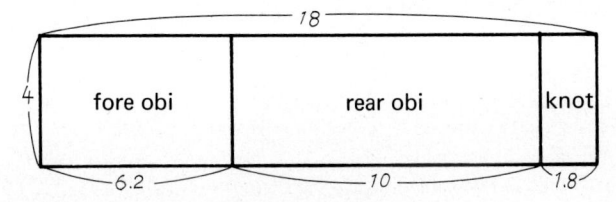

| fore obi | rear obi | knot |

Man carrying a livery coat

Man in a livery coat

Woman with an umbrella

78

Man with a burden

Man with a fan

Man dressed for the Yoshiwara,
the courtesan quarter

Woman with an apron

79

Making the 'Man with a Fan'

[Materials]
Japanese paper for the hair: 2 × 6cm, Kimono: 8.5 × 18cm, Obi: 1.4 × 6cm, Haori: 9 × 15cm, Cord for the Haori: 0.4 × 3cm, Thick paper for the fan: 2 × 3cm.

Making the head Crumple paper down to the width of 1.5cm from 2cm and use it for the back hair. Make it in the same way as the 'Katsuyama'. For the topknot fold paper 1.5cm wide in three and fold the length to 0.7cm. Bring the roots of the hair together and tie then with white cotton thread. Glue this to the rear of the back hair.

Making and dressing the kimono These are the same as for the 'Katsuyama' but no neckband is attached.

Making and attaching the obi Fold the width of the obi in two and attach the fore obi alone.

Making and dressing the haori After folding the haori in four the same way as a kimono, slit it as in diagram 2. Widen out the slit as far as the neckband shoulder opening in the middle of the front of the body. Fold out the neckband to a width of 0.5cm at the hem and 0.2cm at the shoulder opening. Glue both sides from the sleeve hole to under the sleeveband and fold up the hem. Dress the haori on the kimono and after arranging the pose attach the haori cord, and put the fan in the man's hands.

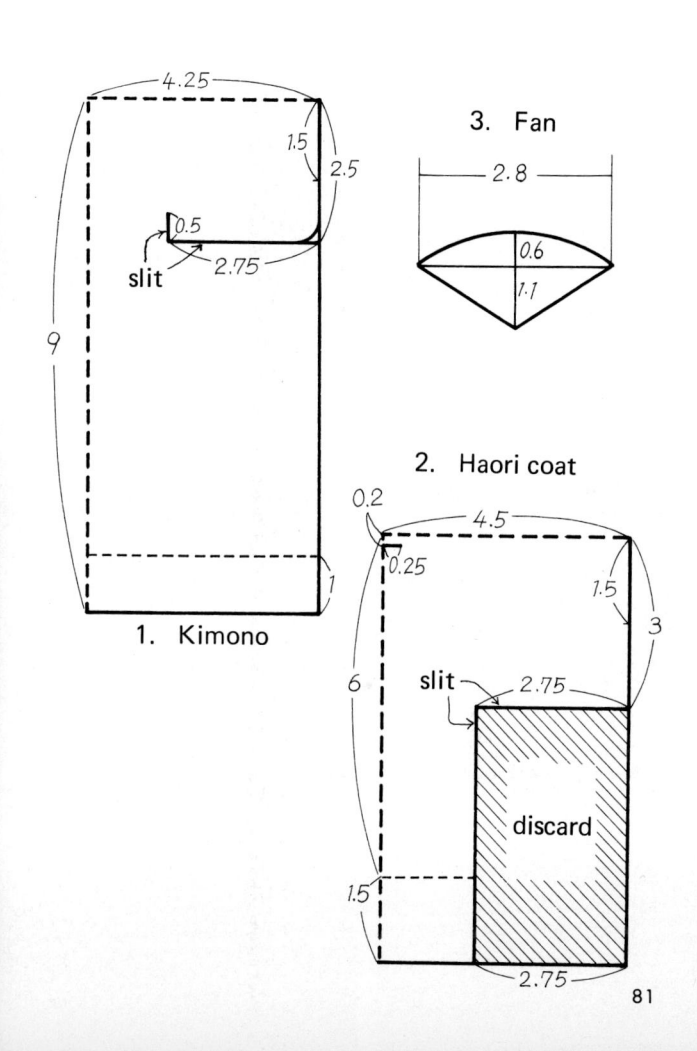

1. Kimono

3. Fan

2. Haori coat

Matching Kimono and Obi with Japanese Paper and the Patterns of Japanese Kimonos

Kimono: Maple and autumn grass pattern
Obi: Small cherry blossoms

Kimono: Maple and autumn grass pattern
Obi: Lotus and foliage

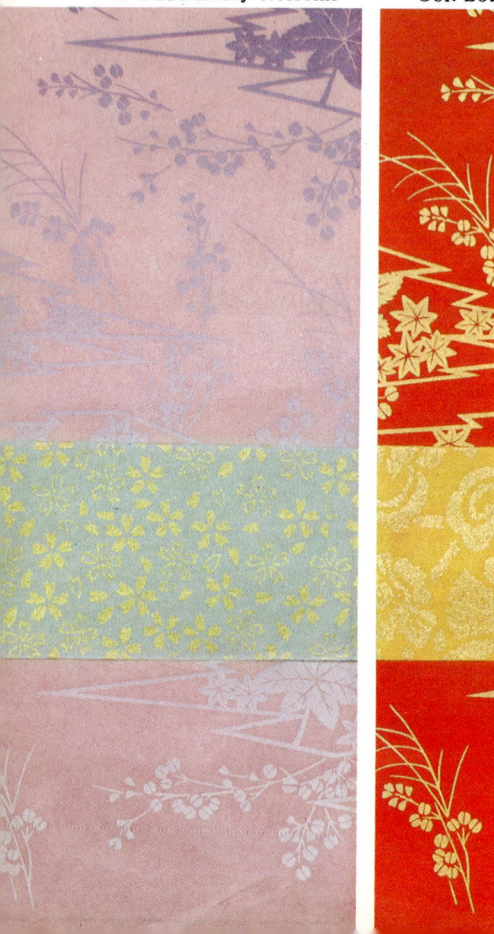

Kimono: Stream and irises pattern
Obi: Lotus and foliage

Kimono: Dapple, basket criss-cross and stripe pattern
Obi: Clouds

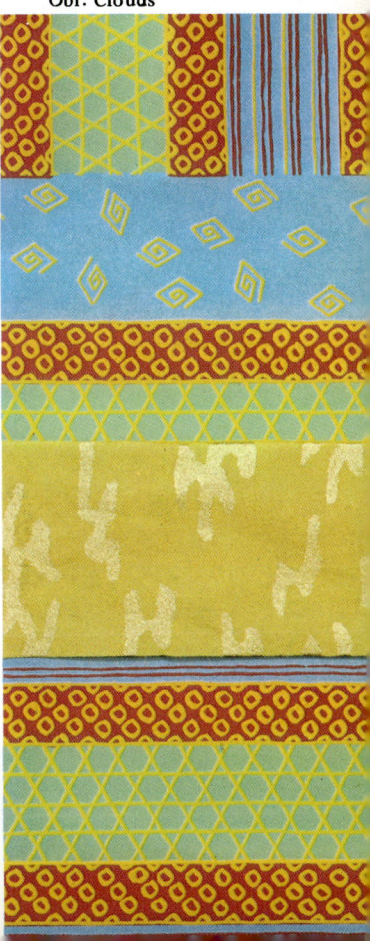

Linked chrysanthemums　　　Bamboo grass design

Cotton print with small flowers

Offset tortoiseshells

Kimono: California
poppy pattern
Obi: Hosoge and foliage

Kimono: Water and irises
Obi: Wild pinks

Kimono: Tortoiseshells
Obi: Hosoge and foliage

Kimono: Water and irises
Obi: Lotus and foliage

Hollyhocks and chrysanthemums

Paulownia design

Resist-dyed (Batik)   Fine stencil-dyed pattern

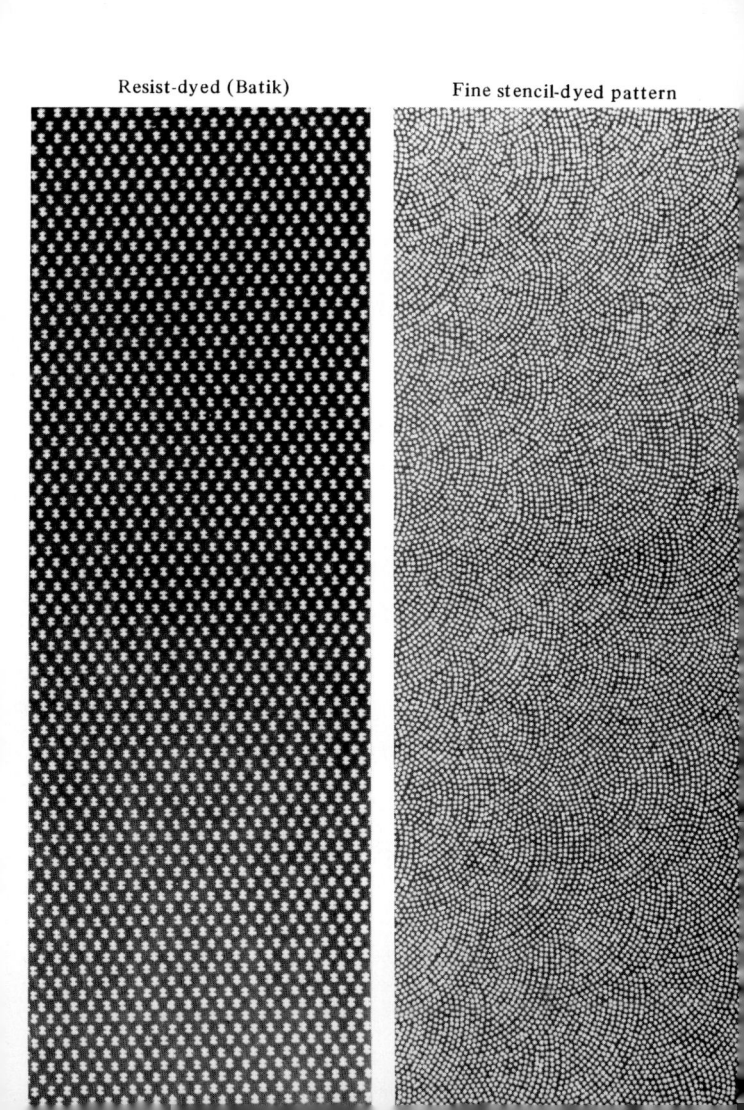

Kimono: Pine, bamboo and plum
Obi: Hosoge and foliage

Kimono: Cherry blossoms
Obi: Hosoge and foliage

Kimono: California poppies and tortoiseshell
Obi: Lotus and foliage

Kimono: Trailing cherry
Obi: Small cherries

Chrysanthemums and cherry blossoms on a snowdrop pattern

Trailing plum and fans

Mist and grasses   Mountains in the mist

Kimono: Double cherry
blossoms on a fence
Obi: Small cherry blossoms

Kimono: Pines and sailing boats
Obi: Small cherry blossoms

Kimono: Chrysanthemums and foliage
Obi: California poppies and tortoiseshell

Kimono: Stream and cherry blossoms
Obi: California poppies and tortoiseshell

Landscape design

Summer and autumn fence design

CONTENTS

Japanese Folk Paper Dolls 98

Making Large Dolls in detail 100

One-Woman Show 116

Paris Exhibition 121

Appendix: Japanese Paper Shops 124

Japanese Folk Paper Dolls 'Anesama'

'Anesama' in the past seem to have been made wherever you went in Japan and they survive at present as the local toys of each district. When I went to Kurashiki in June 1974, just at the time the willows were beautiful, nearly 30 kinds of 'Anesama' were exhibited at the Toy Museum. After my return to Tokyo therefore I immediately requested the publishers and had photographs taken of the dolls. I like local toys and assiduously collected them by buying whenever I had the opportunity until about 1965, but I almost never buy them now since the ones I want are in the main completed.

'Anesama' – Komatsu

'Anesama' with this kind of shape were made in ordinary families. The face and hair are of sweet-corn bark. The doll is rounded and appears finished. However, since they are usually made of thin white paper, the back hair is bigger and flatter. The face is made from folded thin paper without the insertion of cotton padding.

'Anesama' – Matsue, Shimane prefecture

According to the explanation on the box this doll was put in, the Matsue Anesama caught the attention of Koizumi Yakumo – the writer Lafcadio Hearn – and, so it says, was sent to England.

The doll appears to be with a head dress since many large paper hairpins are inserted in the hair. The face is of clay painted with Chinese white and both the hair and the kimono are of paper. The kimono is of horizontal red and green stripes painted by a thick brush, and the dressing is simple. The obi is not shut. In the face the nose protrudes a little with Chinese white, the eyes and nose being gaily painted in by brush. Since the facial appearance is showy, I think it a good thing that the kimono is simple.

Making Large Dolls in Detail (example: Standing Hyogo on page 2)

[Essential Tools] – **refer to the photograph**
Upper right: double hair clip, single hair clip. From the right: tweezers, scissors, thick brush (diameter 0.9cm), medium brush (diameter 0.7cm), narrow brush (diameter 0.5cm), ruler, black cotton thread, wood glue. (Ballpens or pencils may be used instead of brushes.)

[Materials] – **refer to the following pages**
Black Japanese paper for the hair (When you have no black Japanese paper for the hair you may use thin white paper painted black.). Patterned or solid colour Japanese paper for the kimono, the lining, the underclothes, and the obi. White or coloured buffed paper for the lining, the underclothes, the replaceable neckband, and the under petticoat. Thin white paper for the face and under-sash. Cotton wool for the face and torso. Thick paper for the paper pattern.

[Preparations] – **refer to page 102**
In diagram 1, use A for the face and the under-sash, and in B bind together the cotton wadding to insert in the shoulders. Use C to wind round the neckpart. The thickness of the cotton wool of B and C in diagram 2 is half that of A.

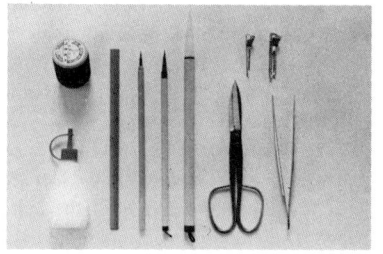

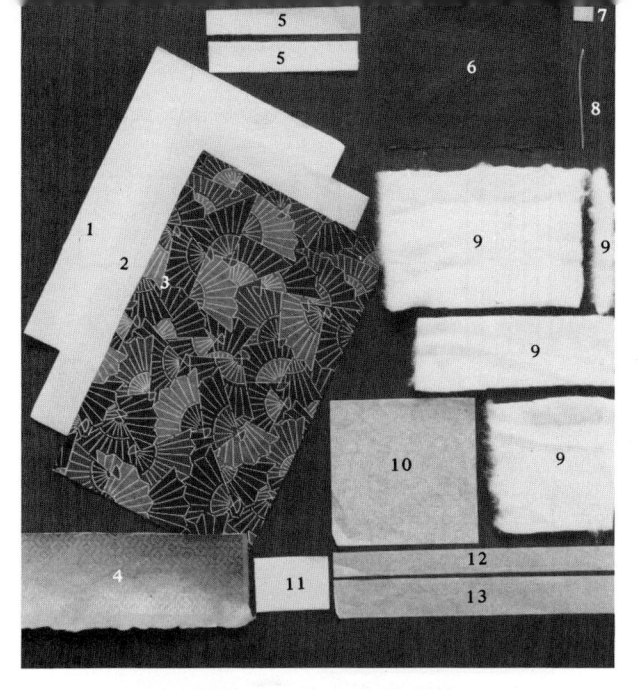

1. White buffed paper for the underclothes
2. Coloured buffed paper for the lining
3. Patterned Japanese paper for the kimono
4. Patterned Japanese paper for the obi
5. White buffed paper for the replaceable neckband
6. Black Japanese paper for the hair
7. Thick paper for the comb
8. Paper braid for the ornamental hairpin
9. Cotton wool for the face and torso
10. Thin white paper for the face and under-sash
11. White buffed paper for the under petticoat
12. Thin white paper for the neck
13. Thin white paper for the face

1. Cutting thin white paper
   - about 36
   - about 26
   - Ⓑ Ⓑ
   - Ⓒ Ⓒ Ⓒ Ⓒ Ⓒ
   - Ⓐ Ⓐ Ⓐ Ⓐ
   - 6 equal parts
   - 4 equal parts

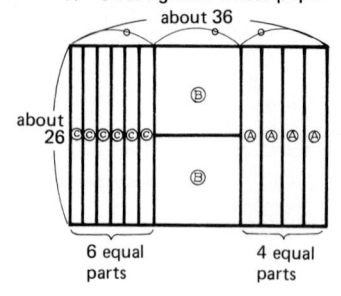

2. Cutting cotton wool
   - 15
   - 12
   - Ⓐ
   - 12
   - 5 Ⓑ
   - 10
   - 10 Ⓒ

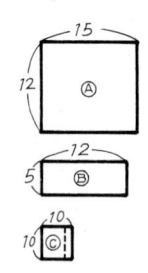

3. Measurement for hair
   - topknot | loop — 6
   - forelock
   - back hair — 6
   - 12
   - 16

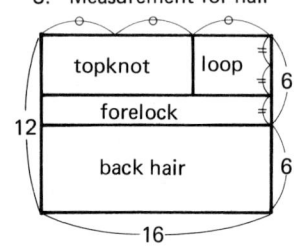

4. Cutting the comb
   - 1.5
   - 0.8
   - 0.1 0.1

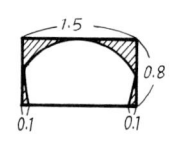

5. Pattern A
   - 1.8
   - 10
   - 9.5
   - 8
   - 11.5
   - 22
   - 8
   - 5.5

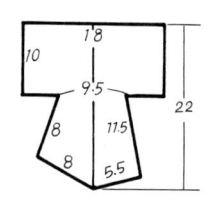

6. Measurements for obi
   - 14, 15, 3
   - 2.7, 2.7
   - 12.5
   - 7
   - 2
   - fore obi | rear obi | knot

102

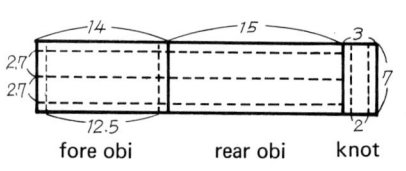

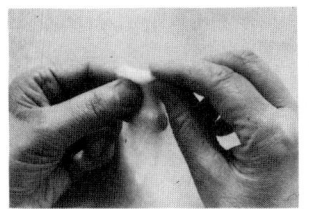

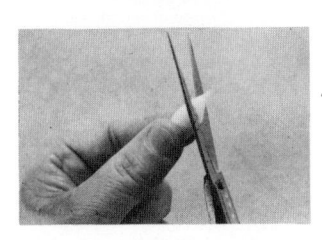

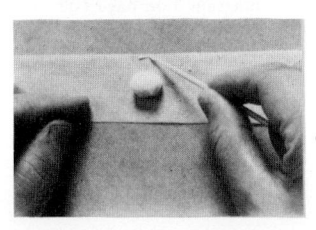

Making the 'Standing Hyogo'

The face

1. Cut the cotton wool C along the dotted line to the width of 1.3cm, and fold one third of the length towards you. Make 0.3cm of the side in a loop into a wick and wind round the cotton wadding.

2. Wind it round well, firming it up, and make it into a spindle shape.

3. Cut the shape of the head with scissors.
4. Chamfer the edges and arrange the shape.

5. Put the cotton wool for the face in the centre of the thin white paper A and glue one side of the paper.
6. Wrap the cotton wadding with the paper A, and glue it.

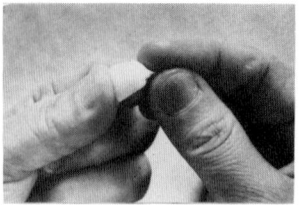

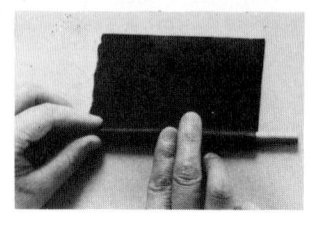

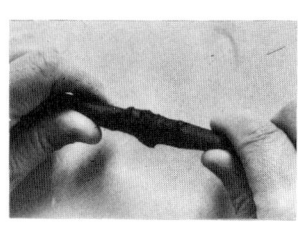

7. Fit the cotton wadding to the paper A, bring it together in the middle at the back and make it into twisted paper string.
8. Do the same for the forehead and chin. The finishing measurements are of about 0.9cm in width and 1.3cm in length.

The head

1. Wind black Japanese paper, 16 × 12cm, around a medium brush. Wind it loosely at first.

2. Crumple the paper by pressing to the middle.
3. Remove the brush, widen out and extend the paper to its full size. Repeat this three or four times and cut up the crumpled paper to the measurements in diagram 3 on page 102.

4. Wind the paper for the back hair tightly round a medium brush, and crumple up the 5cm or so left from winding to a width of 3cm.

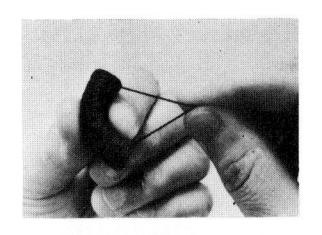

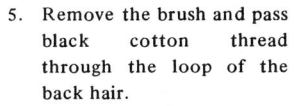

5. Remove the brush and pass black cotton thread through the loop of the back hair.
6. Make the back hair round as you draw in the thread.

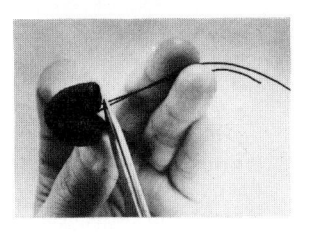

7. Arrange the loop, tie it with the thread, and cut it.
8. Adjust the shape with tweezers.

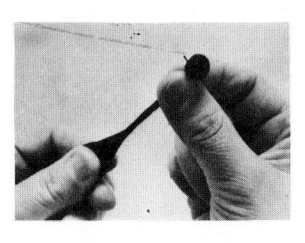

9. Use a thin brush for the forelock and crumple it up to the same essentials as the back hair. Leave 7cm from winding. Pass through cotton thread and tie it at the back.
10. Make the part left from winding into twisted paper string. 
11. Fold the width of the topknot paper into three, insert a medium brush at around one third of the length and fill out the topknot.

12. Fold the place for the root of the topknot in three.

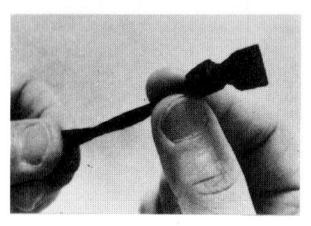

13. Fold the paper for winding to about 0.7cm in width and wind the place for the root of the topknot. Glue the end of the winding.
14. Make the lower part of the topknot into twisted paper string.

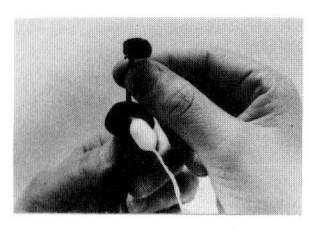

15. Insert the twisted paper string of the forehead side of the face into the back hair.
16. Insert the twisted paper string for the forelock.

17. Insert the twisted paper string for the topknot.
18. Fold the thin white paper C into two and wind the head, but wind it first about three times without inserting the twisted paper string for the jaw side.

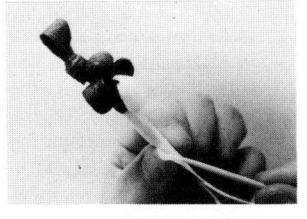

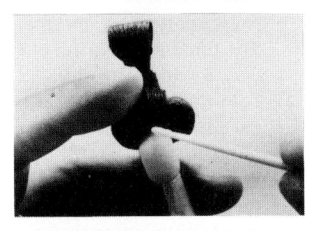

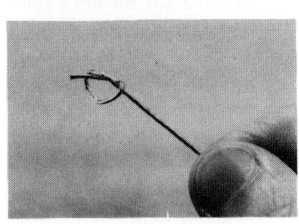

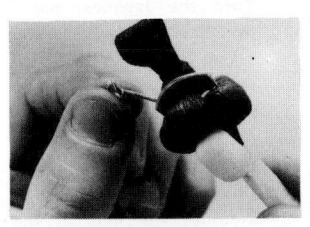

19. Insert the twisted paper string for the jaw and wind it. Wind the paper string downwards naturally and glue it.
20. Draw out the various twisted paper strings inserted in the back hair and adjust the shape.

21. Glue the forehead and fix the forelock. Make the comb from gold paper stuck onto thick paper and cut it as in diagram 4 on page 102.

22. With a single knot in the silver coloured paper braid make a small loop. Pass the paper forward through the loop once more and adjust the loop in a circle, so making the ornamental hairpin.

23. Glue the lower part of the comb and insert it in the back of the forelock.
24. Glue the ornamental hairpin referring to the photograph.

107

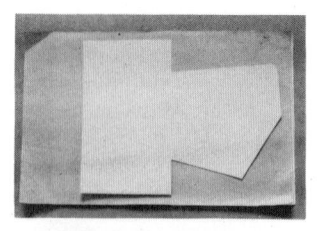

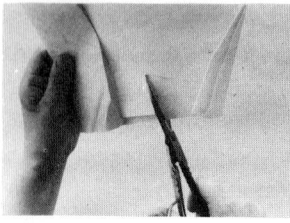

The kimono
1. Make the paper pattern A in diagram 5 on page 102 from thick paper. Place the paper which will be the lining and the paper for the underclothes, each 27 x 18cm, on top of each other back upwards, and rest paper pattern A on top. The folding margin for the hem is 1cm.
2. Fold the upper half, that is the part for the upper half of the body.
3. Fold the two sides of the hem.
4. Insert a slit on both sides under the sleeve.
5. Fold the neckband lining on both sides.
6. Fold both on top the part of the hem previously folded in 3 with the neckband lining folded in 5 underneath it.
7. Turn the Japanese paper for the kimono, 27 x 18cm, upside down and take a fold margin for the hem of 1cm. Rest it on the items folded from 1–6.
8. Fold the top of the kimono, the hem at the foot, and the diagonal hem at the corner.

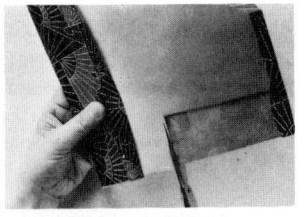

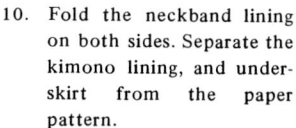

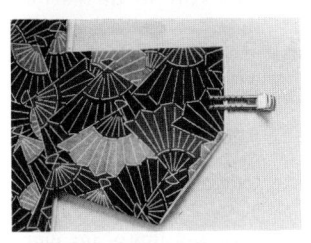

9. Insert a slit under the sleeve.
10. Fold the neckband lining on both sides. Separate the kimono lining, and underskirt from the paper pattern.

11. Mesh together the hems of the kimono and lining at their respective inner and outer skirts.
12. Push out the hem so about 0.2cm shows and fix it with a double hair clip.

13. Glue the neckband lining and stick together the kimono and the lining.

14. Fold back the upper part of the kimono to the neckband width of 0.8cm.

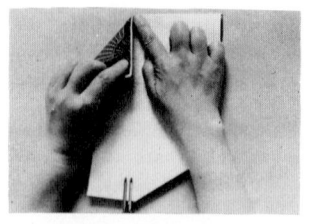

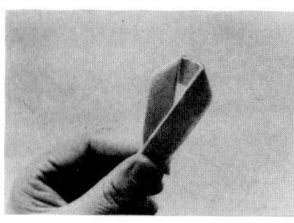

15. Fold the hem of the underskirt in a triangle, push out the underskirt hem a further 0.2cm and put it on top of the kimono. Reset the hem with the double hair clip.
16. Refold the lining and underskirt to fit the fold ridge of the kimono neckband. Fold the neckband to the middle of the body width.
17. Widen the neckband shoulder opening 1cm, and fold the outer skirt neckband. Do this so that the neckband tips of the inner and outer skirts rest on top of one another.
18. Prepare two replaceable neckbands, 13 × 2.5cm, and fold the width of each in two. Rest one on top of another and fold them in readiness to fit the neckband shoulder opening of the kimono.

The torso

1. Wind the cotton wool A on page 102 to the neck, 2cm beneath the doll's chin.
2. Further wind on top the cotton wool B.
3. The photograph shows the torso as wound.

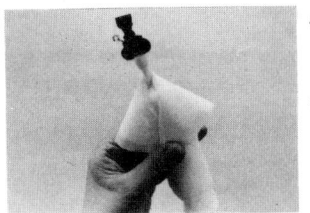

4. Place the cotton wool C on top of the thin white paper B and fold into a triangle.
5. Put the shoulder cotton wadding onto the torso folded in a triangle, in such a shape that the kimono can be dressed.

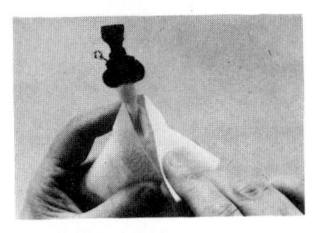

Dressing the kimono
1. Dress the replaceable neckbands one at a time.

2. Dress the kimono so that the replaceable neckband shows a little. Adjust the outer skirt.

3. Insert an angled slit in the neckband tip of the inner skirt. Insert the neckband tip of the outer skirt in the slit and settle it down.

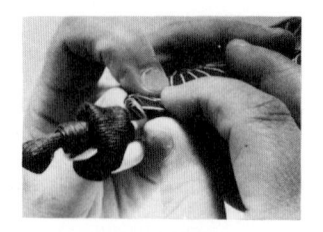

4. Curve outwards the part of the neckband behind the neck, but not too much.

5. Decide the position of the inner neckband shoulder.

6. Decide the position of the elbow and fold it.

7. Adjust the hem of the kimono inwards.
8. After deciding the position of the outer skirt shoulder, fold the elbow of the outer skirt and fold in the tip of the sleeve.

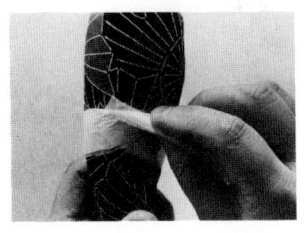

9. Wind in the hem of the inner skirt with the tweezers and arrange the whole.
10. Put about three pieces of the thin white paper C on page 102 on top of one another and make the under sash, amply tighten it with a twist at the back and glue it down.

The obi
1. Fold the width of the rear obi in two, and fold the obi width so that there is a fold margin of 2.7cm at the top and bottom. Also fold the fore obi to the same essentials and fold both ends. Fit the angles of both ends together.
2. Fold the length in two with an overlap interval of about 0.3cm, and also insert just a slight crease in the middle of the width. Take up a pleat with the crease in the centre.
3. Fold the knot to the measurements' width. Take a pleat on the upper side.
4. The parts of the folded-up obi.

Attaching the obi
1. Decide the height of the rear obi, the obi which wraps round the torso, and turn it round from front to back. Cut it leaving part as a glue margin, glue the ends of the obi and fix it to the body.
2. Fold the surplus part to the inside with tweezers so that the obi has a roundness in the middle of the back. Into the obi insert the under sash which protrudes from beneath.

3. Wind the fore obi in readiness with thin white paper at the pleat. Put on the knot from above and glue the rear of the obi.

4. Glue the fore obi to the height in the photograph.

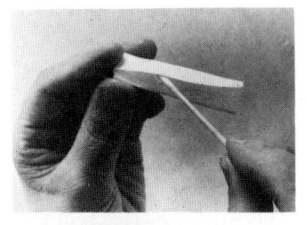

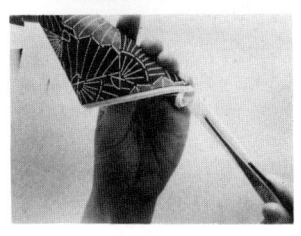

Making and attaching the under-petticoat
1. Fold a 1cm hem on the white Japanese paper of the under-petticoat beforehand. Fold the width in three and mesh it with the hem.
2. Glue the floating part and make a cylinder.
3. Glue the meeting surface of the cylindrical under-petticoat and insert it into the kimono from the hem. Fix it firmly to the back centre. Align the hems of the kimono and under-petticoat.

One-Woman Show

This opened in June 1971 at the gallery of the main Tokyu Department Store at Shibuya in Tokyo. The photographs published here are some of the snaps of the exhibition and of the dolls exhibited. I asked Professor Kubota of the Japan Design School to do the interior design for the exhibition hall. He decorated all the walls with the written characters of the Ballad Drama of the Kantei School, painted on cotton cloth.

The 37 figures of the dolls exhibited were based on the Bunraku puppet drama. In Bunraku the doll operators dress the dolls. Even though it is called dressing the doll there is no body and the women dolls usually do not even have feet. With the replaceable neckband filled with cotton wadding as a base on the wooden torso of the doll, the kimono is fixed by thick cotton thread. After the dressing is completed the wooden neck is inserted to present the finished appearance.

It was a tremendous task for me; even if I knew the measurements for dressing Bunraku dolls, how would I express them in the case of dolls of paper?

Little Maiden and the Demon

This is a very interesting doll which is the first monster in the Bunraku based on Folk Tales by Kinoshita Junji.

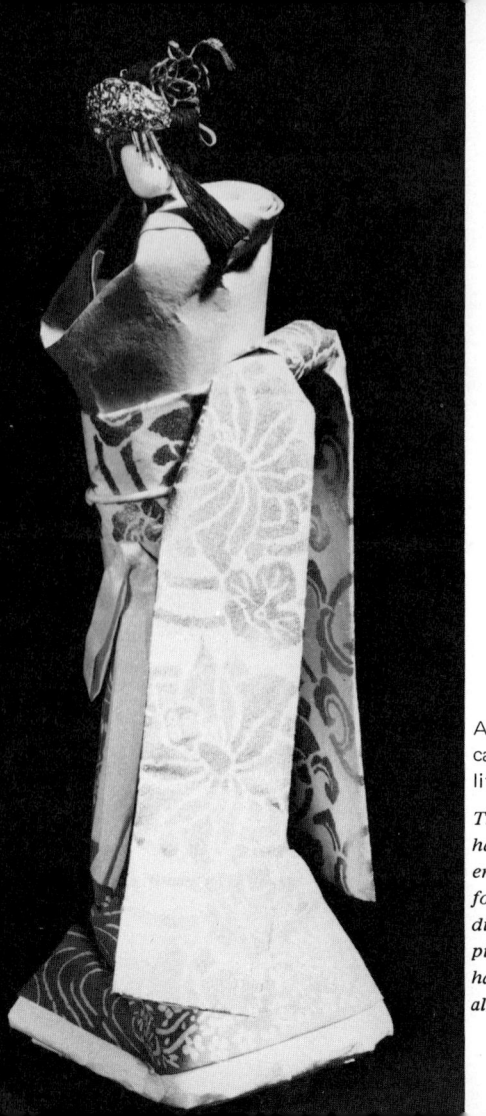

A Young Maiden called Hinadori, the little chicken

The ornamental hairpin of the doll entirely hides the forelock and is quite different to the hairpin in Kabuki. This hairpin is made of aluminium foil.

Osome and Hisamatsu

The garment attached to the neckband of the left doll 'Osome' is called the neckband cover on which is a family crest.

They are the parts of the unwonted lover and the cunning attendant in the story. Since their characters do not show without eyes or nose I have put on the moving eyebrows characteristic of Bunraku.

Yamaya Yasajiro (right) and Kosuke (left)

Paris Exhibition

The 'Exhibition of Japanese Art' was held in Paris for forty days from 16th of March to 23rd of April in 1973, with the assistance of Air France, French Radio and Television, and the Museum of Mankind.

The exhibition hall was the ground floor gallery of French Radio and Television and an exact Nihonbashi in Tokyo with red shrine gates and an arched bridge was set up by French hands.

I was invited to represent paper dolls and together with 50 pupils who went with me we exhibited about 200 dolls in specially installed glass cases. I later heard from someone involved that those admitted during the exhibition reached 200,000 beginning with the splendid reception which welcomed many guests from foreign countries. The exhibition was broadcasted on television whilst it was open and I have also received the news that even pupils living in Brussels were sometimes able to see it.

After the close of the Paris Exhibition the doll section alone was exhibited for a further 30 days at the Nice Folk Art Museum, and later part was contributed to the fund of the Air France Orphanage through the French social welfare organization 'L'Association des allés Brisées'.

Kabuki: Sukeroku

Daffodils

Appendix: Japanese Paper Shops

MORITA JAPANESE PAPER CO., LTD.
Higashi-no-Toin Bukkoji, Shimogyo-ku, Kyoto, 600 Japan

KOBAYASHI at YUSHIMA
1-7-14 Yushima, Bunkyo-ku, Tokyo, 113 Japan

HAKUBUNDO BOOK INC.
1028 Smith Street, Honolulu, Hawaii 96805, U.S.A.

ANDREWS/NELSON/WHITEHEAD
Division of Boise Cascade Corporation
7 Laight Street, New York, N.Y. 10013, U.S.A.

AIKO'S ART MATERIALS IMPORT
714 N. Wabash Avenue, Chicago, Illinois 60611, U.S.A.

JAPANPAPIER IMPORT GESELLSCHAFT, DRISSLER & CO.
6 Frankfurt am Main, Insterburger Strasse 16, West Germany

BERRICK BROTHERS LTD.
20/24 Kirby Street, Holborn, London EC1 N8UA, England

HOIKUSHA COLOR BOOKS

ENGLISH EDITIONS

Book Size 4″×6″

① KATSURA
② TOKAIDO Hiroshige
③ EMAKI
④ KYOTO
⑤ UKIYOE
⑥ GEM STONES
⑦ NARA
⑧ TOKYO Past and Present
⑨ KYOTO GARDENS
⑩ IKEBANA
⑪ KABUKI
⑫ JAPANESE CASTLES
⑬ JAPANESE FESTIVALS
⑭ WOOD-BLOCK PRINTING
⑮ N O H
⑯ HAWAII
⑰ JAPAN
⑱ BUDDHIST IMAGES
⑲ OSAKA
⑳ HOKUSAI
㉑ ORIGAMI
㉒ JAPANESE SWORDS
㉓ GOLDFISH
㉔ SUMI-E
㉕ SHELLS OF JAPAN
㉖ FOLK ART
㉗ TOKYO NIKKO FUJI
㉘ NATIONAL FLAGS
㉙ BONSAI
㉚ UTAMARO
㉛ TEA CEREMONY
㉜ PAPER DOLLS
㉝ JAPANESE CERAMICS
㉞ MODEL CARS
㉟ CREATIVE ORIGAMI
㊱ Z E N
㊲ KIMONO
㊳ CHINESE COOKING
㊴ KYOGEN
㊵ NOH MASKS
㊶ LIVING ORIGAMI
㊷ SHINKANSEN
㊸ OSAKA CASTLE
㊹ BUNRAKU
㊺ TOKYO SUBWAYS
㊻ GIFT WRAPPING

COLORED ILLUSTRATIONS FOR NATURALISTS

Text in Japanese, with index in Lation or English.

Book Size 6" × 8"

BUTTERFLIES of JAPAN

INSECTS of JAPAN vol.1

INSECTS of JAPAN vol.2

SHELLS of JAPAN vol.1

BIRDS of JAPAN

ROCKS

ECONOMIC MINERALS

HERBACEOUS PLANTS of JAPAN vol.1

HERBACEOUS PLANTS of JAPAN vol.2

HERBACEOUS PLANTS of JAPAN vol.3

SEAWEEDS of JAPAN

TREES and SHRUBS of JAPAN

MOTHS of JAPAN vol.1

MOTHS of JAPAN vol.2

SHELLS of JAPAN vol.2

FRUITS

ECONOMIC MINERALS vol.2

FRESHWATER FISHES of JAPAN

GARDEN PLANTS of the WORLD vol.1

GARDEN PLANTS of the WORLD vol.2

GARDEN PLANTS of the WORLD vol.3

GARDEN PLANTS of the WORLD vol.4

GARDEN PLANTS of the WORLD vol.5

THE FRESHWATER PLANKTON of JAPAN

MEDICINAL PLANTS of JAPAN

VEGETABLE CROPS of JAPAN

SHELLS of the WORD vol.1

SHELLS of the WORD vol.2

THE MARINE PLANKTON of JAPAN

EARLY STAGES of JAPANESE MOTHS vol.1

EARLY STAGES of JAPANESE MOTHS vol.2

FOSSILS

WOODY PLANTS of JAPAN vol.1

WOODY PLANTS of JAPAN vol.2

BRYOPHYTES of JAPAN

- LICHEN FLORA of JAPAN
- NATURALIZED PLANTS of JAPAN
- DISEASES and PESTS of CULTIVATED TREES and SHRUBS
- DISEASES and PESTS of FLOWERS and VEGETABLES
- Coloured Guide of Wild Herbs with Artifical Key to Their Families
- THE NEW ALPINE FLORA of JAPAN vol. I
- THE NEW ALPINE FLORA of JAPAN vol. II
- THE LAND SNAILS of JAPAN
- JAPANESE CRUSTACEAN DECAPODS and STOMATOPODS vol. I
- JAPANESE CRUSTACEAN DECAPODS and STOMATOPODS vol. II
- THE LIFE HISTORIES OF BUTTERFLIES IN JAPAN vol. I
- THE LIFE HISTORIES OF BUTTERFLIES IN JAPAN vol. II
- THE LIFE HISTORIES OF BUTTERFLIES IN JAPAN vol. III
- THE LIFE HISTORIES OF BUTTERFLIES IN JAPAN vol. IV
- THE COLEOPTERA OF JAPAN vol. I
- THE COLEOPTERA OF JAPAN vol. II
- THE COLEOPTERA OF JAPAN vol. III
- THE COLEOPTERA OF JAPAN vol. IV
- Colored Illustrations of The Marine Fishes of Japan Vol. I
- Colored Illustrations of The Marine Fishes of Japan Vol. II
- SPIDERS OF JAPAN IN COLOR
- Colored Illustrations of Mushrooms of Japan Vol. I
- Colored Illustrations of Mushrooms of Japan Vol. II
- Ornamental Tropical Plants of the World Vol. I

⟨NEW COLOR PICTURES⟩

Book Size 7″ × 10″

Guide to Seashore Animals of Japan
with Color Pictures and Keys, Vol. I
Guide to Seashore Animals of Japan
with Color Pictures and Keys, Vol. II

(A Forthcoming Book)

The Encyclopedia of Wakan-Yaku
(Traditionals Sino-Japanese Medicines)
with Color Pictures VOL. I, II